What people are sayi

Now Is Not the Time

Bowden combines erudition with remarkable readability. *Now Is Not the Time* is an eloquent call to embrace the flow of time, lest our hasty judgments obscure our understanding of the present.
Nelly Lahoud, US Army War College, author of *The Bin Laden Papers*

How should we think about the relationship between past, present, and future? Brett Bowden offers an erudite and insightful answer. At once a meditation on the character of historical analysis and a pointed challenge to the manifold dangers of presentism, *Now Is Not the Time* is a welcome addition to scholarship.
Duncan Bell, University of Cambridge, author of the award-winning *Dreamworlds of Race: Empire and the Utopian Destiny of Anglo-America*

Like Saramago's *Blindness*, this book reminds us of the absences in our gaze at time, history, and the present. It offers an important contribution to humanity, eloquently and persuasively arguing for a deeper appreciation of vision and time and therefore our lives and impacts on this planet. A beautiful book about the importance of seeing thoughtfully.
Maria Bargh, Professor of Politics and Māori Studies, Te Kawa a Māui, Victoria University of Wellington Te Herenga Waka

I was drawn into the vortex from the outset with this notion of tempocentrism. It made me wonder if I do have a skewed or even deluded perspective about the world as I experience it.

Am I biased? Should I compare this moment to those that have come before? And how can I possibly make any judgement on what is still to come? So many new questions, meaning perhaps *Now Is (Not) the Time* to contemplate so much more.

Leigh Radford OAM, President, Royal Geographical Society of South Australia

We privileged Western humans treat time like a commodity – we want to save it, freeze it, reverse it perhaps, or more usually, speed it up. We are obsessed with a small chunk of history, our history, from which the West emerges preeminent, satisfied. *Now Is Not the Time* takes the obsession with the present to task for its lack of context and historical perspective, its universalism and arrogance. Thinking with big history, and thinking in ways that are disconcerting for moderns, Brett Bowden's powerful book prompts us to ruminate on the problem of tempocentrism as one that is political and imperial. It raises profound questions for people working across many disciplines of the sciences, social sciences, and humanities. Engaging and quick, this is however, a slow burning and bold intervention which will unsettle and provoke readers for a good while after they finish the final page.

Erika Cudworth, De Montfort University, co-author of *The Emancipatory Project of Posthumanism* and *Posthuman International Relations*

Now Is Not the Time

Inside Our Obsession with the Present

Now Is Not the Time

Inside Our Obsession with the Present

Brett Bowden

IFF
BOOKS

London, UK
Washington, DC, USA

CollectiveInk

First published by iff Books, 2024
iff Books is an imprint of Collective Ink Ltd.,
Unit 11, Shepperton House, 89 Shepperton Road, London, N1 3DF
office@collectiveinkbooks.com
www.collectiveinkbooks.com
www.iff-books.com

For distributor details and how to order please visit the 'Ordering' section on our website.

Text copyright: Brett Bowden 2023

ISBN: 978 1 80341 675 5
978 1 80341 684 7 (ebook)
Library of Congress Control Number: 2023946882

A CIP catalogue record for this book is available from the British Library.

Design: Lapiz Digital Services

UK: Printed and bound by CPI Group (UK) Ltd, Croydon, CR0 4YY
Printed in North America by CPI GPS partners

We operate a distinctive and ethical publishing philosophy in all areas of our business, from our global network of authors to production and worldwide distribution.

Books by Brett Bowden

The Empire of Civilization: The Evolution of an Imperial Idea
9780226068145; 9780226142401; 9780226068169

Civilization and War
9781782545712; 9781782545859; 9781782545729

The Strange Persistence of Universal History in Political Thought
9783319524092; 9783319848990; 9783319524108

Direct Hit: The Bombing of Darwin Post Office
9781925078848

Hurtle Clifford Bald
ISSN 2204-6771

Australian Political Parties in the Spotlight (with Dean Jaensch and Peter Brent)
9780975192559

Civilization: Critical Concepts in Political Science, 4 volumes (editor)
9780415469654

The Role of International Law in Rebuilding Societies after Conflict: Great Expectations (co-editor with Hilary Charlesworth and Jeremy Farrall)
9780521509947; 9781107406643; 9780511530517; 9780511576478

Terror: From Tyrannicide to Terrorism (co-editor with Michael T. Davis)
9780702235993

Global Standards of Market Civilization (co-editor with Leonard Seabrooke)
9780415375450; 9780415459853

Berkshire Encyclopedia of World History, second edition, 6 volumes (associate editor with William H. McNeill senior editor)
9781933782652

For my mother, Miriam (Mim) Dawn Bowden

Contents

Preface

This is a relatively short book, but it has taken quite a long time to write. It is about six or seven years since I first put pen to paper, fingers to keyboard actually. For this book, in particular, that is not a bad thing; there is no rush, time is not of the essence, quite the contrary, actually. If this book took another five or ten years to finish, it would not change anything. A decade from now, we might formally be in a new geological epoch, the Anthropocene, but the central argument about our overwhelming need for a now that matters will still hold. Five or ten years from now, we will still be making arguments for why now, the present, is somehow uniquely special and will go down in history as a time of great significance. That is, until some other people living in a "future now" look back (or forward) on that same time and argue that it pales into insignificance compared to the events and changes that are going on in their new "now." There is a good chance it will be some of the same people on each occasion. The cycle will go on. Sure, there will be eras and events that stand the test of time, which we look back on as truly significant, not just a few years later, but decades and even hundreds of years later. However, there will be many more that are nothing more than a footnote, if they are remembered at all, despite the claims made about them at the time. If this book did have a best before date, for whatever reason, a forthcoming election or an imminent conflict, then the point I am making would be a moot one.

It is not actually correct to suggest that I have spent the past six-odd years writing this book. I have not. There were extended periods when the manuscript lay idle, including for a year or more at a time. In that time nothing happened to change my train of thought when I picked it up again, and neither should it have for a subject such as this. The cause for the longest hiatus was the return of an eye disease that poses some challenges for someone in my line of work. Despite the best efforts of ophthalmologists and retinal surgeons, the challenges persist. Visual impairment might be an impediment in many situations, but it need not affect one's perspective, especially their broader historical perspective. This book relies on having a deep historical perspective, rather than the short-sightedness that restricts one's vision and attention to the now that is before them.

Further disruption and interruptions in the past few years were caused by a pandemic and associated lockdowns; during which time my partner and I became responsible for home schooling our two primary school-aged children. Writing could wait, and it did. As ever, students, primary and tertiary, come first. Straddling before and during COVID-19 has been rather interesting in terms of thinking and writing about the issues addressed in this book. No doubt, the disruptions caused by the pandemic are very much real; just how significant they turn out to be and the extent to which the pandemic changes the shape of "business as usual," time will ultimately tell. Many professions and practices are urgently getting back to some form of "normal," or a slightly revised version of normal. The higher education sector is desperate for the return of international students, while also keen on getting back to face-to-face in the classroom or lab. Despite this urge, I for one have instituted a long-term change that precludes a return to the old normal in that I now live 1500 kilometres from my nominal place of work. This opportune change of scenery was timely and fortuitous in terms of moving to a jurisdiction where lockdowns were less frequent and less onerous. However, it is not all thanks to the pandemic; it is more about managing inadequate eyesight, although the pandemic did serve as a timely instigator in thinking about the future and prompting a new normal for my own working arrangements.

For many leaders and commentators, the COVID-19 pandemic represented another unprecedented event, despite the precedents — think influenza pandemic of 1918–1920 or the Black Death plague of the mid-fourteenth century. Universities in Australia and elsewhere have found it to be a particularly testing time, thanks largely to lost revenue streams generated by international fee-paying students. A consequence for the higher education sector in Australia was that universities collectively cut as many as 27,000 jobs in one year, quite possibly more (Hare 2022a). Given the supposedly unprecedented nature of the crisis, university leaders identified it as a problem, rather than as an issue or a situation. Sometimes, issues or situations pass with time, or we adjust to them; they might even resolve themselves. Problems, on the other hand, require solutions. Vice Chancellors earning large salaries, one million dollars a year or more, cannot be seen to be doing nothing. Passivity is not an option. Watching and waiting will not do. It is assumed that prompt and decisive action will save the sector from even greater crisis and so, 27,000-plus people lose their livelihood as universities rebalance their staffing profiles. That is to say, 27,000-plus people were made redundant or, in the case of casuals, did not have contracts renewed.

I am not suggesting these decisions were necessarily right or wrong. University leaders did what they thought needed doing. What I am suggesting, is that treating the pandemic's impact on student enrolment numbers as an unprecedented crisis that requires an urgent solution will likely lead to a particular course of action. Treating it is an unfamiliar situation that requires close monitoring to see how it evolves over time will likely lead to a different outcome, possibly one that involves no drastic decisions or actions. Taking a little time allows decision makers to put events into historical perspective, and this means more than simply looking back and comparing numbers over the past triennium. The broader point here is that this is not just an exercise in abstraction or a thought experiment; treating too many issues as unprecedented and demanding an urgent response has consequences.

Not long after I wrote the preceding passages, barely a fortnight in fact, many of Australia's universities began to reveal record surpluses for the year in question, more than AU$5.3 billion in total, with the largest being in excess of AU$1 billion. Some universities actually increased their international enrollments in 2021 thanks to students' willingness to learn online from offshore (Hare 2022b). So, perhaps not so much a crisis as an unfamiliar situation. Would it have hurt to wait a little while to see how the situation played out? Probably not.

The hasty cross-country shift of home in early 2021 meant that instead of being in lockdown, as was the case in 2020, I was able to undertake a long-delayed end-to-end trek on the Larapinta Trail in remote central Australia. The trail takes its name from the dialect of the local indigenous Arrernte people, Larapinta being their name for the Finke River. The Finke, or Larapinta, is thought to be one of the oldest rivers on planet Earth, dating to approximately 350–400 million years ago. Geological evidence indicates that the river predates the end of the Alice Springs Orogeny, a 150 million year-long tectonic event that concluded approximately 300 million years ago. It seems entirely appropriate, then, that the title for this book, *Now Is Not the Time*, came to me on the fifth day of the walk while descending a tricky stretch of rocky trail passing through a visibly ancient yet timeless landscape. One cannot help but notice and feel the age of the lands through which the Larapinta Trail passes; its ancient geology is something to behold and wonder. Despite my best efforts to set aside thoughts of work and other distractions, I am grateful that this ancient setting offered up a title much more eloquent than the working title that sat uncomfortably at the top of the page. I am also grateful for my walking companions, who, by good fortune, included a chemist, two teachers and a student, along with two very able and knowledgeable guides. Erica, India, Michael, Catherine, Liv, and Damien proved to be engaging interlocutors when the topic of the book came up.

For better or worse, the ideas outlined in this book have not been shared or discussed as widely as they might usually have. This is in part due to working remotely and in part due to travel restrictions brought about by the pandemic. Personally, I have not missed long haul travel at all and have found that to be a blessing in disguise. The planet appears to be similarly grateful for the reprieve. I have, however, had the good fortune for the past six years to teach a cohort of wonderfully engaging Master's students undertaking my History of Ideas class, all of whom, aware of it or not, have helped to kick the project along. The fact that those students have come from such varied disciplines as medicine, communications, design, engineering, history, international relations, literature, music, philosophy, political science, psychology, religion, and teaching has proven to be of great benefit all-round. I am also particularly grateful to a number of anonymous reviewers who provided thoughtful and constructive comments on earlier drafts of the manuscript.

I am particularly indebted to two successive Deans, Peter Hutchings and Matt McGuire, who have been more than accommodating in helping to make the necessary adjustments to my working arrangements that allow me to continue in the job with the appropriate degree of flexibility. Some long-standing friends have stuck with me through thick and thin, spanning continents, oceans, and time zones and for that, I am most grateful: thank you to Kim, Andy, Greta, and Marit. The same goes to Emily, Daren, Alex, and Will, across even more continents and time zones. Closer to home, I am particularly fortunate to enjoy the support and friendship of Victoria, Michael, Elsie, and Hugo. Closer to home again, thanks to my son I have recently had the good fortune to get to know Jarrod,

Sally, Eleanor, Clayton, Dusty, Harry, and Lucy; a big family with big hearts for whom nothing is too much trouble.

As ever, I am eternally grateful for the love and support of my partner, Gerda, and our children Elke, and Lucien. Gerda, also known as Dr Roelvink, is a first-rate scholar, and she has long been an ideal sounding board for ideas, providing thoughtful comments on the manuscript. When it comes to keeping things in perspective, there can be no better catalyst or corrective than the (sometimes-brutal) honesty of children. The foster children who pass through our doors emphatically reaffirm this, a humbling experience if ever there was one.

As I was revising sections of this book in the early part of 2023, I became aware that there are other ways in which now is not the time. Rather cruelly, I watched on as my mother began to suffer from a form of sudden onset dementia. Quite abruptly and quite literally, for her, now was no longer the present, and at times, here was no longer here either, it was somewhere else. More often than not, my mother returned to living in the past, asking about the wellbeing and whereabouts of her own mother and siblings, most of whom have long since passed.

I guess there are times when we all, willingly or otherwise, transport ourselves to another time and place. Back in time, perhaps, to an era when we were more comfortable and felt more at home with our world. Or maybe forward in time to an imagined place where things will look better and brighter than they do now. Fortunately, most of us have the capacity to snap out of daydreams and return to the realities of the present; or for some, it might not be so fortunate. For others, like my mother and the many like her, their own mind no longer permits such options. Now is no longer here, it is somewhere else, another time and place. I dedicate this book to her, my Mum, Miriam Dawn Bowden (nee Williams).

1

The Moment between Two Eternities

Like many people, I have one of those friends who likes forwarding to anyone and everyone in their contacts list any bit of internet advice that comes their way. One particular nugget of wisdom from some years ago sticks in my mind: "Yesterday is history. Tomorrow is a mystery. Today is a gift. That's why it's called the present." Catchy as it might be, that is not why it is called the present. Such advice about "living in the moment" abounds; a quick Google search offers up, "The Art of Now: Six Steps to Living in the Moment," or "10 Tips to Start Living in the Present Moment," and "How to Live in the Present Moment: 35 Exercises and Tools," among much similar advice. Apparently, living in the moment is the secret to happiness and success. Except, for most people, it probably is not. Like a lot of such sayings or phrases, while it might sound catchy, even pithy, it is not particularly sound advice for living your life by. Sure, there might be something in the sentiment worth exploring further, but the secret to a contented life is not hiding in a slogan.

It is also worth noting that for every catchy phrase, there is often another that contradicts it: "Look before you leap" versus "She who hesitates is lost"; or, "The pen is mightier than the sword" versus "Actions speak louder than words." Then, of course, there is Janis Joplin, who was prepared to go against the live in the moment advice by trading all her tomorrows for just one more yesterday so that she could spend another day with her beloved Bobby McGee.[1] Furthermore, what of me and my kind, historians, archaeologists and the like? Are we to be written off as lost causes because we dwell in and on the past, the raison d'être of a profession summarily dismissed?

Perhaps not surprisingly, it was a Baltic German scientist, Karl Ernst von Baer (1792–1876), with a particular interest in embryology, itself a kind of boundary in the stages of life, who elaborated on the idea of the "moment as the border between the past and the future" (Herzog et al. 2016; Baer 1862). One of the more interesting quotes that pops up about living in the present moment comes to us courtesy of Henry David Thoreau (1817–1862): "The meeting of two eternities, the past and the future…is precisely the present moment." As with many literary quotes, this too is plucked from the page without context. Extracted and abridged to suit a particular pithy purpose. Taken from "Economy," the first chapter of *Walden*, in this case, Thoreau is giving his readers an update on what he has achieved during his two years, two months, and two days of solitude in the woods near Walden Pond. Offering just a "hint at some of the enterprises…cherished," and seeking "pardon for some obscurities," he writes: "In any weather, at any hour of the day or night, I have been anxious to improve the nick of time, and notch it on my stick too; to stand on the meeting of two eternities, the past and future, which is precisely the present moment; to toe that line" (Thoreau 1966: 11).

While it sounds nice lyrically, the idea of the present being a meeting point between two eternities, the past and the future, was thought by many to be just that, a lyrical idea. For in the same year in which *Walden* was first published (1854), on the other side of the Atlantic the eminent mathematician, William Thomson (1824–1907), later Lord Kelvin, read a paper before the Royal Society of Edinburgh in which he stated, "I conclude that Sunlight cannot last as at present for 300,000 years" (Thomson 1857: 80). By his calculations, the clock was counting down on the future of humankind, and he was convinced "that the end of this world as a habitation for man, or for any living creature or plant at present existing in it, is *mechanically inevitable*" (Thomson 1855: 94). Thomson's calculations on the age of the

Earth similarly left him confident that "consolidation cannot have taken place less than 20,000,000 years ago...nor more than 400,000,000 years ago" (Thomson 1862: 161; Burchfield 1990: 69). There was no eternal past and, more concerning, no prospect of an eternal future. Rather, planet Earth was thought to have formed somewhere between 20 million and 400 million years ago, which put his thinking at odds with some of his fellow scientists of the time, including those influenced by Charles Darwin's theorizing on evolution.

Pronouncements such as those by Lord Kelvin, a future President of the Royal Society, gave some scientific credence to longstanding beliefs in Christian Europe that the end of the world was indeed nigh. While he did not necessarily believe it so, the American geologist, Thomas Chrowder Chamberlin (1843–1928), observed some decades later, "We have grown up in the belief that the earth sprang from chaos at the opening of our era and is plunging on to catastrophe or to a final winter in the near future" (Chamberlin 1908: 5). Both time's beginning and time's end, then, were thought to be much closer to the present moment than is now known to be the case. That is, we now know the age of the Earth to be around 4.54 billion years old, while the slightly older Sun will continue to burn for at least that long again, possibly as much as 10 billion years into the future according to recent calculations. Lord Kelvin was partially right, though, in that the increasing intensity of the Sun will ultimately render Earth uninhabitable in the extremely distant future, about 1 billion years from now, assuming nothing too serious goes wrong in the meantime (Gesicki et al. 2018; Christensen-Dalsgaard 2021). The general idea that time's end was closer than time's beginning, the ratio of time ahead to time past ever diminishing, might well be a source of the live in the moment dictum. The collective equivalent, perhaps, of the mid-life crisis.[2]

2

Past, Present, and Future

In the wake of the Second World War and the ongoing turmoil that was engulfing Europe, Hannah Arendt (1906–1975) observed in "The Gap between Past and Future" that there are moments when we "become aware of an interval in time which is altogether determined by things that are no longer and by things that are not yet. In history, these intervals have shown more than once that they may contain the moment of truth" (Arendt 1961: 9). The truth, or the significance of the present, and the relationship between past, present, and future, if there is a relationship (or relationships), is one that has intrigued humankind, or some of us at least, for many centuries. Writing around the years CE 397–8, Saint Augustine of Hippo (CE 354–430) mused at some length on the subject of time in Book XI of his *Confessions*, concluding, "it is abundantly clear that neither the future nor the past exist, and therefore it is not strictly correct to say that there are three times, past, present, and future." Rather, he thought it might be more accurate to assert "that there are three times, a present of past things, a present of present things, and a present of future things." To Augustine's (1961: 269) way of thinking, the "present of past things is memory; the present of present things is direct perception; and the present of future things is expectation." Given that the present is widely conceived of as the junction point between past and future, it is not altogether surprising that the present should figure so prominently in our thinking on such matters.

Come the late twentieth century, in considering the different ways in which we might experience modernity, Reinhart Koselleck (1923–2006) again touched on some similar themes in his musings on time, noting that the series of essays on which he was working "will constantly ask: how, in a given present, are the temporal dimensions of past and future related?" For Koselleck (2004: 3), this question "involves the hypothesis that in differentiating past and future, or (in anthropological terms) experience and expectation, it is possible to grasp something like historical time." As Koselleck went on to explain, the idea of historical time, if it has any "specific meaning, is bound up with social and political actions, with concretely acting and suffering human beings and their institutions and organizations." Despite their different experiences of wartime Europe, like Arendt and Koselleck, Norbert Elias (1897–1990) was also concerned with the human condition, individual and collective. As with Arendt and Koselleck, his thinking on this broad subject led him to considerations of time, declaring, "One might say that past, present, and future, although three different words, form a single concept" (Elias 1992: 42).

A single concept perhaps, but the tripartite components are not necessarily equal partners. For it has been suggested that "for the past couple of centuries the dominant Western regime of historicity has been future-oriented," coinciding with Enlightenment ideas about progress and human perfectibility, with the arrow of time very much pointing toward the future. However, the times they are a-changin', whereby the "orientation has shifted during the last few decades with the future clearly relinquishing its position as the main tool for interpreting historical experience and giving way to a present-oriented regime" (Tamm and Olivier 2019: 1). François Hartog (2015: 8) has gone so far as to argue forcefully that he is not alone in observing "how the category of the present has taken hold to such an extent that one can really talk of an omnipresent present." He has even given this phenomenon a name, "presentism."[3] As Hartog (2015: xiv–xv) explains, we are in the midst of a "collective inability to shake off what is generally called 'short-termism' and which I prefer to call 'presentism': the sense that only the present exists, a present characterized at once by the tyranny of the instant and by the treadmill of an unending now."

My concern herein is more than just our obsession with the present, the omnipresent present; it is the sometimes implicit, often explicit, assumption that the present is better than the past, and the future; but not just better, morally superior. Some measure of this is not entirely surprising given the widespread faith in the idea of progress, according to which the present should be an improvement on the past, but it is more difficult to explain why the same should hold when it comes to considerations of the future. Moreover, even if one adheres to the general idea of progress in some arenas — technological, social, political — extending that claim to moral superiority is a tricky and problematic subject. Nevertheless, for whatever reason, the present moment, *now*, continues to be a focus of much attention and an important point of reference. As noted, on one level, this is not altogether surprising given that we all live, quite literally, in the present. However, on another level, the present is all-too-often afforded undue significance, privileged over both the past and the future, seemingly for no better reason than we happen to live in it. That is not to suggest that there is not something special about the present, there might well be, but now is not the time to decide whether it is more significant than previous moments, or those still to come. The time for that is later.

Even Hartog (2015: xv) with his heightened sense of wariness about presentism cannot help but see something qualitatively different, unique, about the present present. He recognizes that the historian is well versed in "viewing from afar," and hopes that his chosen tool, the "regime of historicity" will serve him well in "creating this distance, with a view to having a finer understanding at the end of the process of what is close by."

He adds further that, "in a world in which presentism reigns supreme, the historian's place is more than ever among those who," quoting Charles Péguy (1873–1914), "vigilantly watch over the present [*les guetteurs du présent*]" (Hartog 2015: xvii). There is nothing to argue with here, most historians would gladly endorse the sentiment. But then, Hartog (2015: xvii–xviii) notes how for him, the idea of presentism was, at first, "a hypothesis, which came with a series of questions: does our way of articulating past, present, and future have something specific to it, something which makes today's present, here and now, different from previous presents?" He is "convinced" that the answer is "yes, there is something specific about our present," something special that sets it apart from earlier and, possibly future presents. This leads him to his next question: is the current wave of "presentism a *stopgap* or a new *state*?" That is a big question, the short answer is only time will tell. My suspicion is that we will be doing the same well into future presents, supposing that we are living in a time that is fundamentally unique, unprecedented even.

***

If one is out walking in the woods and uncertain of their location, not exactly lost, but unsure of their bearings, then one of the most effective ways of situating one's self is to get to higher ground in order to work out where you are in relation to certain known landmarks — the carpark, or a nearby town, for example. In such a scenario, what one is looking for is perspective on their present location in relation to other locations, with the relational aspect being key to removing the uncertainty. In a similar way, a peak, be it a hill or a mountain, can seem like the top of the world when you are standing on it, that is, until you look around and see that the next peak is higher again, and the next even higher still. The same basic principles apply equally to the temporal domain just as they do in the spatial domain. All too often, now, the present is a peak assumed to be the highest, without taking the time or trouble to look to the past, or speculate on the future, for some much-needed relational perspective.

This book, then, is about the overwhelming tendency to put too much emphasis and significance on the present moment, often without context or historical perspective.

While imprisoned in the Tower of London, Sir Walter Ralegh (1552–1618), often spelt Raleigh, began working on his *History of the World*, where, in the Preface he wrote:

> I know that it will be said by many, That I might have been more pleasing to the Reader, if I had written the Story of mine own times; having been permitted to draw Water as near the Well-head as another. To this I answer, That whosoever in writing a modern History, shall follow truth too near the Heels, it may happily strike out his Teeth (Ralegh 1687: xxxi).

Ralegh had good reason for not wanting to comment too directly on his own life and times, although it did not save him in the end, but he also appreciated that the passage of time afforded one some much needed perspective when assessing the significance of people, places, and events across history.

3

Historicity or Temporality

In exploring the phenomenon he calls presentism, Hartog's (2015: xv) chosen tool is the "regime of historicity," which is "simply a way of linking together past, present, and future, or of mixing the three categories." Here as elsewhere, historicity is all about what actually happened; historical accuracy and authenticity are all-important (see Margolis and Rockmore 2016). Hartog (2015: xvi) prefers "historicity" over "temporality," or "regime of temporality," as he feels the "latter has the disadvantage of referring to an external standard of time, such as...mathematical, or astronomical time." Relationships to time and the measuring of time are important here for a number of reasons, as explored further below, such as moving between scales of time, from historical time to geological time, and vice versa. The key issue explored and exposed here does indeed involve elements of presentism, but presentism does not quite capture all of it. Another term used to describe the circumstances or phenomenon under discussion here is tempocentrism. Neither presentism nor tempocentrism are particularly elegant or eloquent terms, but they do have some currency and have garnered something of a following, particularly the former. That being the case, there is no need to reinvent the wheel.

What is tempocentrism, then, and how does it differ from presentism? As with any term that has centrism as a suffix, it indicates that that particular term or idea is central to considerations and concerns. In this case, temporal matters, that is, time or timing, or more specifically, the present, is the all-important factor around which all other considerations revolve. There is more to tempocentrism, however, than a mere preoccupation with the present, or presentism; it is further marked by a distinctive inclination to compare and judge the past in relation to the present. Moreover, tempocentrism involves the tendency to assume that the present is not only materially and qualitatively different from the past, but it is superior to the past, often morally superior. This tendency is deeply related to the idea of progress; the assumption being that humankind is advancing and improving as we move forward through time.[4] Similar to other centrisms, such as ethnocentrism or Eurocentrism, those displaying tempocentric traits in their thinking and practice are more than likely to be unaware of their own tempocentrism.

Why does tempocentrism matter? It matters for the same reasons that anthropocentrism, ethnocentrism, and Eurocentrism matter; tempocentrism brings with it a skewed perspective on the world, a perspective that is loaded with bias and prejudice. Anthropocentrism, for instance, is the belief that human beings are at the centre of and the most important entity in the world, living or otherwise. This has consequences for humankind's exploitative relationship with the natural world and other species. Ethnocentrism is the habit of judging other ethnic or cultural groups by one's own values and standards, which are assumed as inherently superior. Similarly, Eurocentrism is the tendency to view, interpret, and judge all Peoples through the prism of European or Western culture, history, and values. Like ethnocentrism, Eurocentrism has had and continues to have serious consequences for the way non-Western Peoples are treated, Christian "civilizing" missions and colonial occupation being prominent examples (see Bowden 2009).

At the heart of Eurocentrism is a view of the world, sometimes implied, sometimes explicit, that situates European (particularly Western Europe) culture, history, and values as the universal norm. Not only are they the norm to which other

Peoples' culture, history, and values are compared and judged (and usually deemed inferior), but they are the culture, history, and values that are assumed to be appropriate and aspirational for all Peoples. Eurocentrism, then, is inherently related to the West's Orientalist tendencies in defining and depicting the "exotic East," as identified by Edward Said (2003), both of which are related to the broader European imperial enterprise, which is in part underpinned by the ideas of civilization and universal history. It is a near article of faith that all Peoples can be fitted into the narrative of history on a continuum between a start and an end; all destined to travel the same path and arrive, ultimately, at modernity (Bowden 2017a).

Coming into prominence as a term in the 1920s, Oswald Spengler (1880–1936) captured the essence of Eurocentrism just prior to the First World War:

> The ground of West Europe is treated as a steady pole, a unique patch chosen on the surface of the sphere for no better reason, it seems, than because we live on it — and great histories of millennial duration and mighty faraway Cultures are made to revolve around this pole in all modesty. It is a quaintly conceived system of sun and planets! We select a single bit of ground as the natural centre of the historical system, and make it the central sun. From it all the events of history receive their real light; from it their importance is judged in *perspective* (Spengler 1918: 17).

Spengler's observations came just as the second wave of European imperial expansion was drawing to a close on the eve of the Great War (see Hobsbawm 1987). He went on to observe that this "conceit" had given rise to an "immense optical illusion" whereby ancient histories, including those of China and Egypt, are reduced to the level of "mere episodes," while Europe's own history in the "decades since Luther,

17

and particularly since Napoleon, loom large as Brocken-spectres."[5] This optical illusion is similar to the apparent slow movement of "a high cloud or a railway train in the distance," and yet we have fooled ourselves into believing "that the tempo of all early Indian, Babylonian, or Egyptian history was really slower than that of our own recent past" (Spengler 1918: 17).

Spengler (2015: 17–18) went on to argue that for Europe and the West, the "existence of Athens, Florence, or Paris is more important than that of Lo-Yang or Pataliputra." That is not the case, however, for the rest of the world, so "is it permissible to found a scheme of world-history on estimates of such a sort?" He thought not; for if so "then the Chinese historian is quite entitled to frame a world-history in which the Crusades, the Renaissance, Caesar, and Frederick the Great are passed over in silence as insignificant." In a similar vein, Spengler thought it "ridiculous" to propose that "modern" history constituted a "few centuries" that were by and large "localized in West Europe," while "ancient" history "covers as many millennia" and into which we "dump...the whole mass of the pre-Hellenic cultures, unprobed and unordered, as mere appendix-matter." He questioned why we keep this "hoary scheme" alive when, in effect, it serves to "dispose of Egypt and Babylon" and largely consigns the "vast complexes of Indian and Chinese culture to foot-notes." Furthermore, what of the "great American cultures, do we not, on the ground that they do not 'fit in' (with what?), entirely ignore them?" Spengler thought that the most appropriate description for this Eurocentric "scheme of history, in which the great Cultures are made to follow orbits round *us* as the presumed centre of all world-happenings, is the *Ptolemaic system* of history." The system that he proposed in its place was a "Copernican" model in which there is no "privileged position to the Classical or the Western Culture as against the Cultures of India, Babylon, China, Egypt, the Arabs, [or] Mexico," which are all "separate worlds of dynamic being" in their own right (Spengler 1918: 17–18).

As Robert Textor (2005: 17) notes in his introduction to the collection of essays by Margaret Mead (1901–1978), *The World Ahead: An Anthropologist Anticipates the Future*, this kind of Eurocentrism or ethnocentrism "and tempocentrism are close psychological cousins." It is not surprising, then, that Spengler (1918: 17) also posed the question: "How, *from the morphological point of view*, should our eighteenth century be more important than any other of the sixty centuries that preceded it?" That is the essence of tempocentrism, it privileges the present over the past. It assumes the present is more important than the past, or the future. It assumes that the events happening now are unprecedented and will change the course of history. We can only really make such declarations with any measure of confidence, however, in hindsight.

Francis Fukuyama, for instance, could not see how the liberal democracy into which he was born and grew up with, could be improved upon as a form of government. He insisted that the end of the Cold War marked not just "the passing of a particular period of postwar history, but the end of history as such: that is, the end point of mankind's ideological evolution and the universalization of Western liberal democracy as the final form of human government" (Fukuyama 1989: 4). By presenting his argument in such a universalist fashion, Fukuyama's "End of History" thesis revisited the Enlightenment idea that humanity is constantly progressing toward a particular end. Since Karl Marx (1818–1883) and Friedrich Engels (1820–1895) muddied the waters, there has been debate over precisely what is humankind's ultimate form of politico-socio-economic organization. With the fall of the Berlin Wall signalling the demise of Soviet communism, Fukuyama claimed that the debate was over. For many in the West it was a moment of triumphalism, a knockout victory for capitalist democracy over authoritarian communism. For Fukuyama (1989: 4), it signified something more; it was "an unabashed victory of economic and political liberalism" and marked the "End of History."

Fukuyama (1992: xii) was not suggesting that the "occurrence of events, even large and grave events" have come to an end, but history in the Marxist/Hegelian sense. That is, "history understood as a single, coherent, evolutionary process, when taking into account the experience of all peoples in all times." According to Hegel, on Fukuyama's (1992: xii) rather circuitous and questionable interpretation, this evolutionary process culminated in "the liberal state, while for Marx it was a communist society," and at the end of the day, at the end of history actually, Hegel supposedly had it right. Georg Hegel (1770–1831), in fact, suffered from the same Eurocentric and tempocentric bias as Fukuyama, in that he could not see beyond his own present in believing that the constitutional monarchy of Prussia in around 1830 was the perfect end. As Bertrand Russell (1872–1970) would later observe, the ideas outlined by Hegel in *The Philosophy of History* made for "an interesting thesis, giving unity and meaning to the revolutions of human affairs," but as with "other historical theories, it required, if it was to be made plausible, some distortion of facts and considerable ignorance" (Russell 1996: 705).[6]

In recent times, tempocentrism has taken on some slightly different guises. Although it is still very much about the notion that what goes on in the here and now is somehow unique and qualitatively different to everything that has gone on in the past, at least to the extent that it constitutes a new chapter or new version. What I have in mind here are recently emerged labels such as War 2.0, or Revolution 2.0, or even Africa 2.0 (Southwood 2002). These labels are imbued with claims that relatively recent developments in information and communications technologies (ICT) represent a kind of seismic shift that relegates everything that has gone on prior to the twenty-first century as Version 1.0, while the first decades of the new century are Version 2.0. For instance, in *War 2.0: Irregular Warfare in the Information Age*, Thomas Rid and Marc Hecker (2009) argue that the rise of insurgencies coupled with the rise of the World Wide Web make for "new forms of social war." Today, in the wake of the digital and ICT revolutions, insurgents and counterinsurgents alike must have a media strategy and a public relations department that can harness the power and reach of new media.

In a similar vein, Wael Ghonim's (2012) *Revolution 2.0: The Power of the People Is Greater Than the People in Power: A Memoir*, outlines how the Google executive's anonymous Facebook page helped launch a revolution that was coordinated via social media and ultimately led to the toppling of Egypt's long-time president, Hosni Mubarak. In *Deglobalization 2.0: Trade and Openness During the Great Depression and the Great Recession*, Peter van Bergeijk (2019) analyzes how the rise of populist movements around the globe have led to new waves of anti-globalization sentiments. In the realm of broadcast media, "War 2.0: Blurring the Battlefield," is a *Newsy* special report that looks at how cyber and information warfare are changing the nature of conflict and pose a threat to critical infrastructure and democratic institutions in the United States. Launched from deep within Eastern Europe, the investigative report suggests that "a new Cold War is changing the face of conflict on both a virtual — and physical — battlefield" (Pyatt and Wahl 2018).

This is not a commentary or critique of the substance of the publications themselves; at least two of the books with which I am familiar are indeed thorough and insightful accounts that provide important new perspectives on their topics, in one case a uniquely personal perspective. Similarly, the documentary report, "War 2.0: Blurring the Battlefield," is an example of well-researched investigative journalism that makes for a half-hour of worthwhile viewing. However, war is as old as human civilization (Wright 1965; Eckhardt 1990, 1992; Gat 2006; Bowden 2013), and the means by which it is fought, observed, and recorded have been continually evolving across millennia. The same can be said of revolutions. The use of propaganda and information warfare is not new in times of war or revolt; the means might be different, but the end remains much the same.

The manifestations of this phenomenon are many, from jumping the gun in declaring a pandemic-instigated crisis in higher education, to claims about the nature of warfare, but they also reach well beyond academe. It has recently been highlighted, for instance, that the "art market, like pretty much everything else in our culture, has become all about the here and now" (Reyburn 2023). The result is that even in the tradition-laden world of art, "contemporary art holds sway, reflecting the fast-forward cultural preoccupations of our society." While there will likely always be a market for masters such as Vermeer or Caravaggio, it is increasingly the case that new and younger collectors "regard art from the distant past as remote and irrelevant." Instead, they are "interested in paintings by artists who are under 45, not over 400" (Reyburn 2023).

As discussed further below, the art world is not immune to the "social acceleration" phenomenon, "which profoundly changes human perceptions of the passage of time" (Reyburn 2023; Eckhardt and Bardhi 2020). The role of presentism-cum-tempocentrism in the appreciation and collecting of art means, the "new is going to provide a higher social status" than the old, which will naturally be "reflected in the price as well" (Reyburn 2023). This is a plus for contemporary artists who can make a living while still producing their work, rather than future descendants being the beneficiaries of their estate. One has to wonder, however, what becomes of this art and its monetary value when it is no longer "new?" Will it date quicker than the buyer might hope? Time will tell.

A key point here is that new media and new forms of information technology might prove to be so significant as to dramatically change the landscape of warfare, the global economy, or social and political movements, but now is not the time to be making such determinations or declarations. Whether they represent a Kuhnian paradigm shift or not will only be known for sure with the passage of time, which might mean fifty, one hundred, or one thousand years from now. To suggest in the midst of a process of change, or in the immediate aftermath of an event, that it marks a dramatic deviation from everything that has come prior is to engage in the kind of presentism and tempocentrism that overlooks or denies the importance of the past. Such thinking effectively neglects the significance of Johannes Gutenberg (c.1400–1468) and his printing press, so too the importance of still photography and moving pictures, or other history-making and world-changing technologies, such as gunpowder, the repeating rifle, or the atomic bomb, to name just a few.

This kind of presentism and tempocentrism requires just as much ignorance and arrogance as Eurocentrism. To suggest that the present is somehow temporally superior to the past just because we now live in it is as flawed as claims to superiority on the basis that one was born on this particular patch of ground, or happens to have this particular color skin. Sports commentators are prone to such hyperbole in the heat of the moment — "We have just witnessed the greatest individual goal since..." — but thinking people with time to pause and reflect ought to be able to do better.

4

A Matter of Time

The passage of time and perceptions about time and our relationship to it, including ideas about the past, present, and future are prominent elements in the discussion here. Humankind has an interesting and complicated relationship with time and its passing. We know there are 60 seconds in a minute, 60 minutes in an hour, 24 hours in a day, 7 days in a week, 52 weeks in a year, 10 years in a decade, 100 in a century, and even that is a much larger scale than most of us are inclined to contemplate. Nevertheless, in part because of increasing concerns about climate and environmental crises, even larger scale time frames — with units accounting for tens of thousands or even tens of millions of years — have made their way from various sciences, such as cosmology, evolutionary biology, geology, and palaeontology into the lexicon of not only the humanities and social sciences, but broader public debate. Moreover, despite what we know about the limits of time that are available to us in any given day or lifetime, we are known to try to capture or freeze time, such as through still photography. Some of us are time-poor and try to save time, by cutting corners. While others seek to slow it down or even reverse it with anti-aging remedies, as if aging is unnatural or an illness (see Rabheru 2022).

To a certain extent, then, our experience and understanding of time and its relatability to the everyday is relative, it depends on what one is doing as they experience it or the situation under consideration. As Albert Einstein (1879–1955) is reputed to have said when asked once too often to explain the theory of relativity: "Put your hand on a hot stove for a minute, and it seems like an hour. Sit with a pretty girl for an hour, and it seems like a minute. That's relativity." As is discussed further below, the movement and coming together of ideas and time scales from different disciplinary fields has created some awkward and difficult situations as we, individuals along with communities large and small, try to contemplate and account for the micro and macro near simultaneously. In order to explore this issue further, let us first take a quick look at some ideas about the speeding up and slowing down of time, before moving onto the micro and macro scales of measuring its passage.

Speeding Up

It is with some regret that time to pause is becoming all too rare a commodity; a luxury that too few are afforded or afford themselves.[7] It has been observed and argued for a good while now that the pace of life is speeding up. Koselleck (2004: 22), for instance, notes that "in the eighteenth century, the acceleration of time that had previously belonged to eschatology became obligatory for worldly invention, before technology completely opened up a space of experience adequate to this acceleration." This speeding up of the pace of life and rate of change has been going on for some time then, albeit it unevenly, hitting its straps with the industrial revolution and charging on without too much resistance. As James Gleick (1999) has highlighted, the result is many of us "feel that we're more time-driven and time-obsessed and generally rushed than ever before."[8] In the twenty-odd years since he made these observations, the pace of life and its accompanying machinery have only accelerated further. In fact, one of Gleick's fast machines, the facsimile or fax, is now so immobile and cumbersome that it is effectively going the way of the telex machine and the telegraph sounder before it: obsolete and destined for the museum. The sense that life in general is speeding up is not so surprising when we consider the suggestion by Hartmut Rosa (2013) in *Social Acceleration* that the "speed of human movement from the pre-modern period to now has increased by a factor of 100." If we were to factor in jet-propelled air travel, or space travel, the factor would be significantly larger again. Hot on the heels of the revolution in transport was a revolution that saw the speed of communications rise "by a factor of 10 million in the 20th century" alone. During the same period, the speed of data transmission has rapidly increased "by a factor of around 10 billion" (Rosa 2013; Vanderbilt 2014). Moreover, there is every reason to believe that it will continue to grow exponentially.

Given this sense of time speeding up and the pressures that go with it, it is understandable that adjustments and accommodations have been made to help us cope. We can buy fast food or order it fast delivery, two-minute noodles for lunch or, even quicker, one-minute rice or instant soup washed down with instant coffee, all heated up with fast boil kettles. Smartphones come with speed dialling and fast charging, fast upload and fast download, making it easy to skim through fast news or apply for fast loan approval. Fast lanes are chock full of fast cars racing to speed dating and speed mentoring appointments, while some do not even leave their home or office and do it all online. Even the impatient gardener is catered for with fast growing trees (Brandon 2013).

I do not want to come across as too flippant here; while two-minute noodles might be quick, convenient, and a savior for students living on a tight budget, other aspects of this speeding up have had profound effects on everyday lives. The 24-hour or 24/7 news cycle, for example, is now a fact of life; 24-hour news networks and live news feeds are the new norm in order to keep up with fast-paced lifestyles in cities that never sleep. We can now experience the outside world in "real time," or watch it unfold at least. Newspapers can no longer keep up, the "news" is often out of date by the time the printed paper hits the newsstands. Fast news, however, comes at a cost: with the latest news delivered to your device of choice, speed is of the essence, but often at the cost of accuracy, not to mention depth.

As highlighted more than two decades ago by Kovach and Rosenstiel (1999) in the introduction of *Warp Speed*, in the 24-hour news cycle, the news media is increasingly interested in "ferrying allegations" and less concerned with "ferreting out the truth." In discussing TV news channels in particular, Kansas and Gitlin (1999; 2001: 84) observed at around the same time that they had evolved into "all-chat, much-guesswork, even-more-opinion-and-attitude," rather than reporting on and investigating the "news." As Kovach and Rosenstiel went on to explain (1999: ch. 1), news stories often emerge as "piecemeal bits of evidence, accusation, or speculation" that are sifted through and aired in public as the day proceeds, often requiring clarifications, retractions, or apologies as the "story" unfolds; and then, just as quickly, it is abandoned as a new scandal breaks. The presentation of news has altered dramatically in the time since CNN (Cable News Network) launched in June 1980. The corporatization of news media coupled to an obsession with celebrity means that "commentary, chat, speculation, opinion, argument, controversy, and punditry cost far less than assembling a team of reporters, producers, fact checkers, and editors to cover the far-flung corners of the world." While the news might well be faster and more frequent, constant even, it does not necessarily follow that we are better informed about what is going on in the world. Likewise, just because we can fix a meal in minutes, does not necessarily mean we have a better diet and enjoy better health than some of our ancestors.

Instant Gratification

Both a cause and an effect of the speeding up of the pace of life is the desire for instant gratification, which, while slightly tangential, is worth having a "quick" look at. Instant refers to a very short measure of time and the impending immediate moment, that is, now, the ever-moving interface between past and present. While many of us might bemoan the hectic pace of life, we also do not appreciate having to wait for things that we want now. There is an old adage: What do we want? Instant gratification. When do we want it? NOW! This is the essence of instant gratification, the desire to have a pleasure or benefit fulfilled immediately, even though it is likely to be less rewarding or less beneficial than a future outcome. Related to this urge is the pleasure principle, the generally accepted belief that human beings are driven, to a considerable extent, by a desire to experience pleasure while avoiding pain.

The impulse to seek pleasure and avoid pain has had its evolutionary advantages for our early ancestors, for whom the fight, flight, or freeze instincts were called upon more frequently in confronting the many dangers faced by hunter-gatherer societies than the kind of long-term thinking that is required for retirement planning. Greater long-term thinking became more important with the expansion of agricultural societies that engaged in seasonal cropping plans coupled with food storage (Ray and Najman 1986; Cannon 1915). Nevertheless, the psychologist, Shahram Heshmat (2016), identifies ten reasons why it remains so difficult to forego an immediate good or pleasure instead of holding out for a greater good in the future. The first is a general desire to avoid delays where possible and instinctively embrace opportunities for pleasure as they arrive. The second relates to feelings of uncertainty that can lead us to opt for a certain and immediate good instead of a greater but uncertain benefit down the track. The next concerns the observation that younger people are more likely to be impulsive decision-makers, while the older are more experienced and have developed a capacity to suppress some urges for immediate gratification. Delaying gratification is easier if one has a plan or picture of what their future looks like, without that there is not much of an urge to plan accordingly. Fifth is the related contention that the more intelligent you are, the more likely you are to think about and plan for your future. That, however, might not be practical or possible if immediate circumstances, such as poverty or homelessness, mean having to make choices that meet immediate needs, such as food and shelter, over longer-term benefits. Some people naturally have a greater predilection for impulsive behavior than others do, making them more vulnerable to potentially addictive habits. Similarly, some people have a greater capacity to regulate their emotions, meaning that when confronted with stressful or upsetting situations, they are less likely to resort to immediate options that make one feel better right away, like eating a tub of ice-cream, that might not be in their best interests long-term. There are still times when even people with a heightened ability for emotion regulation can get bored, impatient, or just be in a bad mood, leading to a desire for some form of irresistible immediate gratification. The tenth and final reason concerns feelings of anticipation and how these can affect decision-making; we are more likely to look forward to positive outcomes and seek them as soon as possible, whereas we delay or avoid unpleasant or painful outcomes for as long as possible. Interestingly, the language one speaks and whether it has a conception of the future can have some bearing on our capacity to plan ahead or resist temptation for immediate gratification (Chen 2013; Sutter et al. 2018).

Slowing Down

The sense that life is ever speeding up, then, is not necessarily an unqualified good, nor an unqualified bad, there are upsides and downsides; there are also many unintended consequences, which can also be good, bad, or ugly. Gleick (1999: 110) suggests that this speeding-up began long ago, particularly from the era when we developed an ability to shape and polish glass lenses, giving rise to telescopes, microscopes, spectroscopes, and more, allowing us to see further, smaller, larger, clearer, and then, come the late nineteenth century, "perhaps most important of all – we learned to see faster." Significantly, these instruments allowed us to see the past more deeply, and the present more clearly, both giving hints of the future.

The capacity to see faster was thanks, in large part, to the development of Eadweard Muybridge's (1830–1904) zoöpraxiscope, which made this possible by actually slowing things down and breaking them into smaller moments in time that could be captured on film.

In 1872, industrialist, former Governor of California and future United States Senator, and founder of Stanford University, Leland Stanford (1824–1893), among whose many interests included horse breeding and racing, commissioned Muybridge to produce a portfolio of his properties and prized possessions, including a racehorse named Occident. Stanford was dissatisfied with existing understandings of horses in motion, believing that depictions of galloping horses with all four feet clear of the ground when fully extended fore and aft was incorrect. As such, he also wanted Muybridge to devise a means that could break down the action of a horse at a gallop. A grainy image of Occident at the gallop in 1873 was the first step, which Stanford found encouraging. By mid-1877, Muybridge had produced a much-improved image of Occident at full speed, and in June the following year he used 12 automatically triggered cameras arrayed along the track at Stanford's farm at Palo Alto to capture the images that would become the famous series of cabinet cards, "Sallie Gardner: The Horse in Motion." The images proved Stanford correct; the only time when all four hooves of a galloping horse are clear of the ground is when they come together under the horse (Muybridge 1888, 1893).

The Horse in motion. "Sallie Gardner," owned by Leland Stanford; ridden by G. Domm, running at a 1.40 gait over the Palo Alto track, June 19, 1878. Source: Library of Congress Prints and Photographs Division. https://www.loc.gov/pictures/item/97502309/

This episode served to kick-start chronophotography and the art of moving pictures more generally, at the same time changing the nature of our relationship with the observable world by speeding it up. From that time on, there has really been no turning back or slowing down; communication and data transmission have accelerated, while mass transport has become more readily accessible and affordable. As Gleick (1999: 114) concludes in citing historian Stephen Kern (2003), the "historical record shows that humans have never, ever opted for slower."

Split Seconds

The speeding up of life, including the vehicles in which we travel, and with it perceptions about the passing of time, has meant that many of us are required to be more accountable for our time. This in turn has necessitated that we get better or more efficient at measuring it and capturing it in ever-smaller fragments. At the 2002 United States Formula One Grand Prix at Indianapolis Motor Speedway, for instance, Brazilian, Rubens Barrichello, drove his Ferrari into first place, beating teammate, Michael Schumacher of Germany, by 0.011 seconds. After a race-time of 1 hour, 31 minutes, and 7.934 seconds over a distance of 306.235 kilometres, this was the smallest winning margin in the history of the sport, a matter of mere centimetres. The finish was so close that Schumacher said after the race, "we did not know who had won until we got out of the cars."

On average, the blink of a human eye takes about one-tenth of one second, or 100 milliseconds. Clearly, there was not much in it at the finish, as the saying goes, blink and you would have missed it. Motor sports are not unique when it comes to this kind of obsessing about the measuring of time and breaking it down into ever-smaller pieces. The quantifying, measuring, and assigning of value to time (Time is money!) has become the norm for much of the working world, whether a plumber on a callout, a lawyer reviewing a client's file, or an academic with a workload plan. In a globalized world, albeit unevenly, reliant on high-speed information and communication technology to drive endeavors such as 24-hour trading, along with the rapid movement of all manner of goods around the world by air and sea, the result is a kind of compression of time-space that transforms long-held perceptions about the obstacles posed by time and distance (Harvey 1990).

For much of human history, a knowledge of the changing seasons and the phases of the moon served one well, while later rudimentary devices served their purpose and were close enough. As Willis Milham (1923: 31) notes in his authoritative study of timekeeping, "it is safe to conclude that the sundial was in use in the valleys of the Tigris and the Euphrates at least as early as 2000 BC." More accurate and versatile clepsydra or water clocks followed within centuries (Milham 1923:

48), while the use of candle clocks had become increasingly widespread by the sixth century CE. What we might describe as modern mechanical clocks did not appear until the thirteenth or fourteenth century (Milham 1923: 55), with the minute hand only becoming a regular feature in the late seventeenth century, thanks in large part to Galileo Galilei's (1564–1642) work on pendulums. The third hand, that is, the second hand, first appeared on German clocks in the fifteenth century, but was not commonplace until the eighteenth century and often on a separate sub dial (Orzel 2022). Today, now, mechanical timepieces are becoming something of a rarity, rather, the synchronization of personal devices using satellite technologies and "the cloud," along with synchronization more broadly have become standard practice (Jordheim 2017).

The exactitude of timekeeping has come a long way in a relatively short period. Today, the International System of Units states one "second is the duration of 9,192,631,770 periods of the radiation corresponding to the transition between the two hyperfine levels of the ground state of the caesium 133 atom" (Bureau International des Poids et Mesures 2019). That is very precise indeed, although it really does not mean much to most of us. Like many people, I still use the phrase "wait a sec" or "I'll be with you in a sec" when one of my children calls, "Dad, can you come?" To their annoyance, a sec is always more than one second; it takes me longer than that to get up, or to hit save, or almost anything else one might be doing. For better or worse, such imprecise time measurement and timekeeping is becoming a thing of the past; it certainly is not good enough for Formula One motor racing or many other endeavors where very large sums of money, along with reputations, are at stake.

5

Deep Time

Toward the other end of the spectrum, to split seconds, warp speed, and hyper-globalization is something known as deep time, a term first used by John McPhee (1981) to describe long-term geologic processes in his book, *Basin and Range*. The idea of the *longue durée* is familiar to many historians, with notable early contributions from Marc Bloch (1886–1944), Lucien Febvre (1878–1956), and later Fernand Braudel (1902–1985), all insightfully described by Febvre (1973) as "A new kind of history." Deep time deals with an entirely different order of magnitude (Shryock et al. 2011; Rudwick 2007, 2008, 2016). For as McPhee (1981: 29) notes, "numbers do not seem to work well with regard to deep time. Any number above a couple of thousand years — fifty thousand, fifty million — will with nearly equal effect awe the imagination to the point of paralysis." To demonstrate his point metaphorically, he asks us to "consider the earth's history as the old measure of the English yard, the distance from the king's nose to the tip of his outstretched hand. One stroke of a nail file on his middle finger erases human history." If the concept of deep time is confronting to our sense of time, then the related idea of Big History deals with an even grander scale again, taking in the 13.8 billion years or so from the Big Bang to the present (Christian 2005).

McPhee's discussion of geology and deep time owes much to the Scotsman, James Hutton (1726–1797), referred to by many as the father of geology, and by at least one as the "man who found time" (Repcheck 2009). At two meetings of the Royal Society of Edinburgh in March and April 1785, Hutton revealed his "Theory of the Earth," something he had been working on for a considerable period. Early on, he explained that a key "object is to know the time which had elapsed since the foundation of the present continent had been laid at the bottom of the ocean, to the present moment in which we speculate on these operations" (Hutton 1788: 297). By the end of the second lecture, Hutton concluded:

> We have now got to the end of our reasoning; we have no data further to conclude immediately from that which actually is: But we have got enough; we have the satisfaction to find, that in nature there is wisdom, system, and consistency. For having, in the natural history of this earth, seen a succession of worlds, we may from this conclude that there is a system in nature; in like manner as, from seeing revolutions of the planets, it is concluded, that there is a system by which they are intended to continue those revolutions. But if the succession of worlds is established in the system of nature, it is in vain to look for any thing higher in the origin of the earth. The result, therefore, of our present enquiry is, that we find no vestige of a beginning, — no prospect of an end (Hutton 1788: 304).

It is quite evident from this passage that Hutton was no wordsmith; in fact, his prose was generally rather torturous. As Stephen Jay Gould (1987: 6) notes in *Time's Arrow, Time's Cycle*, even if they could follow his impenetrable writing, the "world was not ready for Hutton" and his Theory of the Earth. As noted above, Lord Kelvin was not convinced either, preferring his own mathematical methods and models for dating the Earth. It was not until almost fifteen years after Hutton's lecture when another Scottish scientist, John Playfair (1748–1819), published *Illustrations of the Huttonian Theory of the Earth* (1802) that Hutton's ideas began to catch on.

Speculation about the geologic age of the Earth, along with ideas about "uniformity in the course of nature" (Playfair 1802: 243), were further popularized with the publication of the first volume of Charles Lyell's (1797–1875) widely available and highly influential, *Principles of Geology* (1830), in which he presented a range of geologic evidence supporting Hutton's theory. Lyell, another Scottish geologist, employed the terms "uniformity of the order of nature," or "uniformity of the course of nature," or just "uniformity of nature" with regularity in the *Principles*. He went on to declare the "establishment, from time to time, of numerous points of identification, drew at length from geologists a reluctant admission, that there was more correspondence between the physical constitution of the globe, and more uniformity in the laws regulating the changes of its surface, from the most remote eras to the present, than they at first imagined" (Lyell 1830: 85–6). The idea of uniformity in nature expounded by Hutton, Playfair, and Lyell was subsequently coined "uniformitarianism" in a review of Lyell's *Principles of Geology* by the English polymath, William Whewell (1794–1866), the man who also gave us the name "scientist."[9] In essence, the idea of uniformitarianism holds that the natural laws and processes that shape the Earth today are the same natural forces that have always acted on the Earth everywhere; that is, they are uniform and universal. Uniformitarianism also inverts the idea familiar to many historians that the past is key to the present, to assert that the present is key to the past, another twist in thinking about the relationship between past, present, and future (Adler and Menze 1997; Rance 1999).

Prior to uniformitarianism gaining traction, it was widely accepted that the Earth was created through supernatural means, possibly no more than six thousand years ago, and had subsequently been shaped by a range of catastrophic events, including the Biblical flood. Championed by the French scientist, Georges Cuvier (1769–1832), this increasingly questioned theory was termed "catastrophism," as also named by Whewell (see Cuvier 1813). In Lyell's (1835: 327) mind, however, "never was there a doctrine more calculated to foster indolence, and to blunt the keen edge of curiosity, than this assumption of the discordance between the former and the existing causes of change."

It was in the same third volume of the *Principles* that Lyell (1835: 385) suggested that it would be "useful to distinguish" the Tertiary period into "four successive periods, each characterized by containing a very different proportion of fossil shells of *recent* species." He termed these four periods, epochs actually, the "Newer Pliocene, Older Pliocene, Miocene, and Eocene." Following on from the Palaeocene (circa 66 to 56 million years ago), the first epoch in the Paleogene Period, the Eocene extended from approximately 56 to 33.9 million years ago (MYA).[10] The Miocene runs from approximately 23.03 to 5.333 MYA, and the Pliocene from 5.333 million to 2.58 million years before the present (BP). The Oligocene Epoch, 33.9 million to 23 million BP, would be identified later. In around 1839, Lyell introduced another epoch, the "Pleistocene," 2,580,000 to 11,700 years ago, in order to distinguish it from the Pliocene. The epoch in which Lyell lived, then known as Recent, the epoch in which we all still live now, was subsequently named the "Holocene" by the French entomologist and palaeontologist, Paul Gervaise (1816–1879), in the concluding passages of a paper published in 1850 (Walker et al. 2009).[11]

As discussed in detail further on, as an example of presentism-cum-tempocentrism at work, the Holocene might well turn out be the briefest epoch in the history of the Earth, given that there are moves afoot to recognize a new epoch, the Anthropocene. Nevertheless, just as McPhee outlined, the dimensions of deep time are difficult for many of us to comprehend with any real sense of proportionality. We have even had to create new acronyms to accommodate such a grand scale: MYA for millions of years ago and BP for before the present, whereby the present is generally recognized as the first day of January 1950, the eve of radiocarbon dating. When it comes to looking way, way back in time by peering out into space with powerful telescopes, we use the term light-years, whereby a light-year is the distance that light travels in an Earth year, which is about six trillion miles or nine-and-a-half trillion kilometres. Robert Macfarlane would later suggest that the identification of eons, which are divided into eras, which are in turn divided into periods, which are in turn divided into epochs, which are in turn divided into ages, demonstrates the "power of language." Supposedly even more powerful than the geological forces they describe. Thus, the "geological past, and hundreds of millions of years," deep time, were rather effortlessly shoehorned into a handful of letters and single-word names (Macfarlane 2003: 53).

While Lyell's work would have a lasting influence on the naming of some of these geological epochs and the need for new acronyms to quantify them, his more immediate impact was on the minds of young scientists, including Charles Darwin (1809–1882). Having barely finished his studies, starting out in medicine before finding his way to natural history, including geology, the 22-year-old Darwin accepted a position aboard the second survey voyage of the *HMS Beagle*, captained by Robert FitzRoy (1805–1865), whom Lyell had asked to collect specific geological samples on the expedition. Just prior to setting off in late-December 1831, Captain FitzRoy gifted Darwin the first volume of Lyell's *Principles of Geology*. The second volume reached Darwin via the mail in November 1832, while the *Beagle* was docked in the port city of Montevideo in Uruguay. The expedition lasted nearly five years, with the *Beagle* returning to England in early October 1836. By the end of October, Darwin and Lyell met for the first time, ultimately becoming close friends, with Lyell helping to facilitate the publication of some of Darwin's research. In a letter to Leonard Horner (1785–1864) in 1844, just two years before Horner was elected President of the Geological Society, Darwin (1903: II, 117) wrote:

I cannot say how forcibly impressed I am with the infinite superiority of the Lyellian school of Geology over the continental. I always feel as if my books came half out of Lyell's brain…for I have always thought that the great merit of the Principles was that it altered the whole tone of one's mind, and therefore that, when seeing a thing never seen by Lyell, one yet saw it partially through his eyes.

Fifteen years later, with the publication of *The Origin of Species*, Darwin (1929: 253) would declare:

He who can read Sir Charles Lyell's grand work on the Principles of Geology, which the future historian will recognize as having produced a revolution in natural science, yet does not admit how incomprehensibly vast have been the past periods of time, may at once close this volume. Not that it suffices to study the Principles of Geology, or to read special treatises by different observers on separate formations, and to mark how each author attempts to give an inadequate idea of the duration of each formation or even each stratum. A man must for years examine for himself great piles of superimposed strata, and watch the sea at work grinding down old rocks and making fresh sediment, before he can hope to comprehend anything of the lapse of time, the monuments of which we see around us.[12]

As Gould noted in making a rather different point, Lyell's *Principles of Geology* ultimately led to the "codification of deep time" on the back of its "compendium of factual information," which, "when extended through deep time," are the drivers of all geological phenomena, "from the Grand Canyon to mass extinctions." It was now possible to reject scientifically the "miraculous agents" required by the dramatically briefer "biblical chronology." Thus, the "discovery of deep time" marked a triumph of "observation and objectivity over preconception and irrationalism" (Gould 1987: 6). In a similar vein, Macfarlane (2003: 53) observed that "anyone who has opened a geology textbook" would recognize that between roughly "1810 and 1870," with the coining of names such as "Precambrian, Cambrian, Ordovician, Silurian, Devonian, Carboniferous, Permian, Triassic, Jurassic, Cretaceous, Tertiary, Quarternary [sic] ..." in effect, "the scale of deep time was constructed and labelled."

Naturally, this recognition did not make science or scientists immune to criticism, even from those from within. Responding rather satirically to what he perceived as the anthropocentrism of evolutionary theorist Alfred Russel Wallace's (1823–1913), *Man's Place in the Universe* (1903), Mark Twain (1835–1910), with a keen interest in science and technology himself, penned the essay, "Was the World Made for Man?" Written in 1903, the year Wallace's book first hit the shelves, but not published until 1962, Twain (1974: 170) concludes by pondering:

> Man has been here 32,000 years. That it took a hundred million years to prepare the world for him is proof that that is what it was done for. I suppose it is. I dunno. If the Eiffel tower were now representing the world's age, the skin of paint on the pinnacle-knob at its summit would represent man's share of that age; and anybody would perceive that that skin was what the tower was built for. I reckon they would, I dunno.

Despite the scientific and wider recognition garnered in the late-nineteenth century and again in the early twenty-first, there is something missing from this narrative. In a similar line of thought to Gleick, Macfarlane (2003: 44) suggests that the "seventeenth and eighteenth centuries had been the centuries when space was extended, when the realm of the visible had suddenly been increased by the invention of the microscope and the telescope." This, however, is only part of the story. For instance, non-Westerners and First Nations Peoples have also been observing the night skies for thousands of years (Selin 2000; Norris and Norris 2009; Noon and De Napoli 2002). While in the realm of earth sciences, particularly geology, as Stephen Toulmin and June Goodfield (1967: 77) observe, when it comes to the "History of Nature, Islamic scientists were beginning to see farther than their predecessors had ever done. Around AD 1000 Avicenna was already suggesting a hypothesis about the origin of mountain-ranges which, in the Christian world, would still have been considered quite radical eight hundred years later."

Abū-ʿAlī al-Ḥusayn ibn-ʿAbd Allāh Ibn-Sīnā (c. 970–1037), more commonly known as Avicenna in the Western world, was an eminent Persian polymath who made important contributions across a range of what we now call disciplines, from astronomy to medicine, and from metaphysics to music. When it came to geology, he proposed:

> Mountains may be due to two different causes. Either they are the effects of upheavals of the crust of the earth, such as might occur during a violent earthquake, or they are the effect of water, which, cutting itself a new route, has denuded the valleys, the strata being of different kinds, some soft, some hard. The winds and water disintegrate the one, but leave the other intact. Most of the eminences of the earth have had this latter origin. *It would require a long period of time for all such changes to be accomplished, during which the mountains themselves might be somewhat diminished in size.* But that water has been the main cause of these effects is proved by the existence of fossil remains of aquatic and other animals on many mountains (quoted in Toulmin and Goodfield 1967: 77–78).

In a somewhat different manner, while still challenging the accepted narrative, is the idea that some Indigenous Peoples have a different sense of time or a different relationship to history than Westerners. For some, it is a history that encompasses much more than the relatively brief span of time since contact with and conquest by Europeans (Griffiths 2018; McGrath and Jebb 2015). The sense of time and place extends beyond human history and, a bit like Avicenna and Hutton, involves reading the landscape to find the stories it can tell about the past. For many of Australia's Indigenous Peoples, for instance, time and place are not so easily distinguished; as custodians of Country, they are also custodians of its songs and stories, its origin stories or creation-time, its Dreaming. Their relationship to the past and the future can also differ; the past is not something that is thought of as behind us, rather it is in front of us, it can be seen a long way back. The future, on the other hand, is unknown and out of sight, it is to the rear (Boroditsky and Gaby 2010; McGrath 2015). As it is for the indigenous Aymara people of the Andes in South America (Núñez and Sweetser 2006). Peter Matthiessen made similar observations about the remote peoples of the Himalaya during his travels in the region as recorded in *The Snow Leopard*. He was struck by how similar their understanding of time and space was to that of certain Native American Peoples in North America. Matthiessen (1978: 53) was also well aware "Australian aborigines — considered to be the most ancient race on earth — distinguish between linear time and a 'Great Time' of dreams, myths, and heroes, in which all is present in this moment." Interestingly, perceptions about the direction of time and its relationship to us is another area where a person's or a community's spoken and written language might have some influence on their orientation (Fuhrman and Boroditsky 2010; Miles et al. 2011; Li et al. 2019).

For those of us more accustomed to thinking in terms of generations, or split seconds, McPhee might be right in suggesting that the contemplation of deep time could potentially bring one to the "point of paralysis." Macfarlane (2003: 43) hints as much when he suggests that in pondering the "immensities of deep time," we are faced with an idea "that is both exquisite and horrifying," in that the present is effectively obliterated as it is "compacted to nothingness by the pressures of pasts and futures too extensive to envisage." Despite this potential for paralysis, or even obliteration, Macfarlane (2003: 44) believes that "there is also something curiously exhilarating about the contemplation of deep time."

The question of scale, or scales of time, has become deeply salient in discussion and debate about the Anthropocene, as elaborated below. With concepts such as deep time migrating from the sciences into the humanities and social sciences, we see the coming together of, at times, incongruent language and objectives. As Dipesh Chakrabarty (2018: 6) explains, the idea of the "Anthropocene requires us to think on the two vastly different scales of time that Earth history and world history respectively involve." For Earth scientists, "the tens of millions of years that a geological epoch usually encompasses," and for social scientists, the "five hundred years at most that can be said to constitute the history of capitalism."

Prior to any such notion of a new geological epoch, in contrast to McPhee's and Macfarlane's take on deep time, in their monumental work, *The Science of Life* (1929), H. G. Wells (1866–1946), Julian Huxley (1887–1975), and Wells' son George Philip (1901–1985), insisted that conceiving of such vast time scales is easier than one might think. In Book 3, Chapter 2, "The Evidence of the Rocks," Wells, the prolific and visionary author best known for his works of science fiction, Huxley, brother of the author, and philosopher Aldous (1894–1963) and grandson of Thomas Henry Huxley (1825–1895), aka "Darwin's Bulldog," and Gip Wells, a distinguished zoologist in his own right, wrote:

Even to-day the average man tends to think the six-thousand year antiquity of Babylon or Egypt enormous. But just as astronomy is teaching us to think of cosmic space on a wholly different scale from geography, to be measured in terms of "light-years" running into ten thousands of millions of miles, so geology is making it necessary to think of earth-history on a wholly different time-scale from human history, in terms of million-year periods, to which a decade bears almost the same proportion as an hour does to a century, and a century as a day does to a whole generation of human life.

To think in such magnitudes is not so difficult as many people imagine. The use of different scales is simply a matter of practice. We very soon get used to maps, though they are constructed on scales down to a hundred-millionth of natural size; we are used to switching over from thinking in terms of seconds and minutes to some other problem involving years and centuries, and to grasp geological time all that is needed is to stick tight to some magnitude which shall be the unit on the new and magnified scale — a million years is probably the most convenient — to grasp its meaning once and for all by an effort of imagination, and then to think of all passage of geological time in terms of this unit (Wells et al. 1931: 199).

So, there we have it, moving between split seconds and deep time is just a matter of imagination and practice, something we can get used to, just as we have with maps; which are now ever-present in our cars and on our smartphones ensuring we do not get lost. Interestingly, in telling the vast origin story of Big History, David Christian compresses a 13.8-billion-year timeline into 13.8 years to give the reader a better sense of the "chronological shape of the story," for he suggests that "natural selection did not design our minds to cope with millions or billions of years" (Christian 2018).

It is difficult to know just how well the deep time scale fits in a world where many of its inhabitants are driven by the need for instant gratification, or where important decision-making is based on weekly public opinion polling and the furthest ahead an elected official plans for the future is the next election cycle. Nevertheless, broadening our thinking in terms of time scales is important. At the very least, having an appreciation of deeper time helps to give us perspective on many important issues, from changes in the climate to changes in currency exchange rates.

6

Naming and Claiming

One of the consequences of our preoccupation with the present and our unwavering belief that we live in unprecedented times marked by monumental turning points in world history is that in the midst of such events or would-be crises, we think them so significant as to require a name, as we do with hurricanes or tropical cyclones. The list of economic, banking, and financial crises, crashes, and panics goes back centuries (for example, Black Monday, Panic of 1825, OPEC oil shock, Asian financial crisis, etc.). As do geopolitical conflicts, disputes, and incidents (e.g. Beagle Conflict, *Baltimore* Crisis, Fashoda Incident, and so on). It is usually not until later, sometimes much later, that we are able to make a more reasonable assessment thanks to the perspective offered by the passage of time. This is all part of the presentist-tempocentric mindset: the present and its crises and crashes, disputes and dilemmas, are like nothing that has come before; they are unprecedented, true turning points in history. Except, often they are not.

The inclination to name things is also about ownership, laying claim to something, be it a mountain, a mouse, a moon, or a moment in time. The identification and naming of eons, epochs, and ages by some of Europe's leading scientists is part of the rush by Europe's exploring powers to "discover," name, and lay claim to the wild and savage world beyond, by force if necessary. This process really gathered pace in the nineteenth century as Europe expanded across the seas and mapped, named, and claimed with abandon, including far off places and peoples, along with periods of time past. As is discussed further below, the idea of the Anthropocene is where presentism-tempocentrism, the rush to name things, and deep time all come together; albeit somewhat ironically, in the process, deep time is actually compressed or truncated.

Eponymy, or the tendency to name things, almost anything, after people, usually men, has been with us for a long time. The Limmu List from Ancient Assyria, for instance, dates to almost two thousand years BCE, recording the names of Assyrian officials after whom each new year was named (Barjamovic et al. 2012). Today, along with lakes, rivers, and mountains; parks, peninsulas, and stars; diseases, ducks, and trees; sofas also have names, pants have names, shoes have names, as do so many other dispensable things (Stoner et al. 2018). Converse's iconic Chuck Taylor All Stars hi-top shoes have been with us for about a century. Chuck Taylors or Air Jordans, however, are not particularly controversial, but when it comes to naming geographical features, new species, or even would-be countries, the landscape is far more treacherous. Even a very brief dip into the field of toponymy, the study of place or geographic names, reveals contentious names such as Rhodesia, named by the British South Africa Company after its founder, Cecil Rhodes (1853–1902), with a capital, Salisbury, named after a Prime Minister of the United Kingdom, Lord Salisbury (1830–1903). While Rhodesia and this particular Salisbury are no more, supplanted by names such as Zimbabwe, Zambia, and Harare, debate still rages about legacies and the propriety of place names and monuments, including the many dedicated to Rhodes.

During his wide-ranging discussion of mountains, and the surveying of Mount Everest in particular, Robert Macfarlane (2003: 189–90) makes the insightful point that "with mapping came naming." As he highlights, the "nineteenth century, more than any other, saw the wild places of the world being franked and hallmarked." When it comes to Mount Everest, I suspect that most people know that, with an elevation of 8,848.86 metres, or 29,031.7 feet, it is the highest peak on the planet. Many are also aware that Edmund Hillary and Tenzing Norgay were the first climbers to reach the summit of the mountain on May 29, 1953. Some are also aware of the attempt to summit the mountain by George Mallory (1886–1924) and Andrew Irvine (1902–1924) in June 1924, which ultimately cost them their lives. What, however, of the mountain the Tibetans call *Qomolangma* (sometimes recorded as *Chomolungma*)? Or the mountain the Nepalese call *Sagarmāthā*? Or the mountain the Chinese named *Zhūmùlǎngmǎ Fēng*? These are in fact, all the same mountain. The mountain we call Everest.

As the British Surveyor General of India during the 1940s, and a long-serving member of the Great Trigonometrical Survey, Andrew Scott Waugh's (1810–1878) intention was, whenever possible, to adopt a local name for significant landmarks, but which one? As he later reported to the Royal Geographical Society of London (1857: 346):

I was taught by my respected chief and predecessor, Colonel Geo. Everest, to assign to every geographical object its true local or native appellation. I have always scrupulously adhered to this rule....

But here is a mountain, most probably the highest in the world, without any local name that we can discover, or whose native appellation, if it have any, will not very likely be ascertained before we are allowed to penetrate into Nepal and to approach close to this stupendous snowy mass.

In the mean time the privilege, as well as the duty, devolves on me to assign to this lofty pinnacle of our globe, a name whereby it may be known among geographers and become a household word among civilized nations.

In virtue of this privilege, in testimony of my affectionate respect for a revered chief, in conformity with what I believe to be the wish of all the Members of the scientific department, over which I have the honour to preside, and to perpetuate the memory of that illustrious master of accurate geographical research, I have determined to name this noble peak of the Himalayas "Mont Everest."

The man himself, George Everest (1790–1866), was not particularly taken with the idea; he had not seen the mountain and believed Everest would be difficult for the people of India to pronounce, moreover, it did not translate well into Hindi. Nevertheless, the name Mount Everest persists (Keay 2000). As Macfarlane (2003: 189) notes, the European obsession with "naming was a form of commemoration." At the same time, it was also very much a form "of colonization: a thwarted expression of the Victorian drive to bring the Empire home." The urge to collect, accumulate, and show off exotic samples, "which reached its fullest expression in Britain with the Great Exhibition of 1851 — didn't work as well with mountains as it did with, say, flora and fauna." The same goes for people for that matter, who were not off limits when it came to bringing home trophies to show-off. So, in order to show where they had been and staked a claim, they resorted to leaving "their names behind. It was a form of imperial graffiti" (Macfarlane 2003: 190).

Iconic as Mount Everest might be, there are recent examples of other iconic geological features reverting to earlier local or indigenous place names. The great monolith in central Australia that for more than a century was formally known by the name Ayers Rock, is now known as Uluru / Ayers Rock. The name Uluru comes from the language of the local Pitjantjatjara People and is thought not to have any particular meaning in the Pitjantjatjara dialect, nor an English language equivalent. The English name for the rock comes from Sir Henry Ayers (1821–1897), then Chief Secretary of South Australia, and was given to the rock by the explorer-surveyor, William Christie Gosse (1842–1881), when he came upon it on July 19, 1873. One hundred and twenty years later, on December 15, 1993, the rock was officially given the dual name, Ayers Rock / Uluru, with both names being equally recognized and used either together or individually. Then, on November 6, 2002, the name of the rock was formally changed to Uluru / Ayers Rock, reversing the dual name order.[13]

North America's highest mountain peak, Denali, has undergone a similar name changing process. The mountain has long been known to the native Koyukon Peoples as *Denali* (or *Dinale*), essentially meaning high or tall, but in 1896, in the midst of a presidential election, a gold prospector named it Mount McKinley after the then-presidential candidate and soon-to-be president, William McKinley (1843–1901). The United States formally adopted the name when the Mount McKinley National Park Act passed into law in 1917, but the name never really caught on in Alaska and in 1975, the Alaska Board of Geographic Names formally named the mountain Denali. On August 28, 2015, the rest of the United States caught up with the state of Alaska when the name Mount McKinley was dropped in favor of Denali.[14]

Despite the end of the age of exploration and imperial expansion here on planet Earth, the search for new frontiers, new species, new resources goes on at pace, from the forest floor to the sea floor, and from the petri dish to the far reaches of space (Bowden 2020). As noted, accompanying this endeavor is the continuing urge to name new discoveries, events, inventions, and things in general after notable people. Hence, along with the Hubble and Webb space telescopes, named respectively after the astronomer Edwin Hubble (1889–1953) and the NASA Administrator James Webb (1906–1992), are the David Attenborough plesiosaur, *Attenborosaurus conybeari*, and the Beyonce horse fly, *Scaptia beyonceae*. The list is a long, constantly growing, and not always distinguished one.

While names like Attenborough, Hubble, Everest, or McKinley might not be as controversial as Rhodes or Stalin,[15] the habit of laying claim to things by naming them has quite a fraught history right up to the recent past. For instance, in 2005, the International Astronomical Union (IAU) named a crater on the dark side of the Moon after the Nobel Prize winning Hungarian-born German physicist, Philipp Lenard (1862–1947). Lenard received the Nobel Prize for Physics in 1905 for his work on cathode rays and his wider contributions to the photoelectric effect. Not far from the crater named after Lenard was another crater named after another Nobel Prize winning German physicist, Johannes Stark (1874–1957). The IAU named the crater after Stark in 1970 in recognition of his 1919 Nobel Prize in Physics "for his discovery of the Doppler effect in canal rays and the splitting of spectral lines in electric fields," otherwise known as the Stark effect. However, as was realized all too late by the IAU, both Stark and Lenard were committed Nazis, enthusiastic followers of Hitler, and strident anti-Semites who led the attack on fellow Nobel Prize winning physicist, Albert Einstein (Ball 2014; Lenard and Stark 1996).[16]

The far side of the moon no longer has craters dedicated to Stark and Lenard, with their names formally being removed by the IAU on August 12, 2020.[17] When naming things, then, authorities need to do their background research and be very sure of the character and integrity of the person they are memorializing, or it could come back to haunt them. They also need to make sure that the feature in question does not already have a name. Equally, when giving an event or would-be crisis a name, such as a panic in financial markets, we should be a little more circumspect before declaring a hiccup or "market correction" a fill-in-the-space crisis. There is only room in the calendar for so many Black Mondays (1987, 2020), Black Tuesdays (1929), Black Wednesdays (1992), and so on.

Know Thyself

There are two specific episodes in the history of naming that are particularly noteworthy here; the first concerns ourselves, that is, the naming of our own species, *Homo sapiens*. The evolutionary history of modern humans is a fascinating topic, one that is the subject of much debate, considerable uncertainty, and regular updating with each new archaeological discovery. Our species acquired the name *Homo sapiens* in 1758 when the Swedish naturalist and taxonomist, Carolus (or Carl) Linnaeus (1707–1778), responsible for formalizing binomial nomenclature, offered a lengthy description of *Homo sapiens* in the tenth edition of his *Systema Naturae* (1758: 20–24). Alongside the entry Homo is the Latin phrase, "nosce Te ipsum," which translates as "Man, know thyself." In essence, *homo* refers to human beings, while *sapiens* means wise or knowledgeable. As Earle Spamer (1999: 112) states in his contribution to a debate about human lectotypes, "The name *Homo sapiens* means 'wise man' or 'knowing man'."

Homo sapiens are rather unique in that there is no specific type specimen, that is, a single physical example, or illustration for that matter, held in a collection anywhere in the world associated with the species. However, as Spamer (1999: 112) notes, this is no great scandal, for the "matter of *Homo sapiens* is peculiar only in Linnaeus's (and our) 'intuitive' understanding of these taxa — that is, knowing ourselves — so not surprisingly none of Linnaeus's 'study specimens' of this species were set aside for future reference." In other respects, *Homo sapiens* might not be quite so unique as initially thought when it comes to being wise and knowing, for it is becoming increasingly evident that Neanderthals shared many of our traits. And yet, *Homo neanderthalensis* or *Homo sapiens neanderthalensis* are named after the valley, Neandertal, or Neander Valley in English, in the German state of North Rhine-Westphalia where the first specimen to be identified was found (Pääbo 2014; Wragg Sykes 2020; Skov et al. 2022).

So too, *Homo floresiensis*, sometimes referred to as the "Hobbit," is named after the island of Flores in the Indonesian archipelago where it was discovered in 2003 (Brown et al. 2004). Another member of the genus *Homo*, the *Denisovans*, still awaiting a taxonomic name because of a scarcity of confirmed finds, is similarly named after the Denisova Cave in Russian Siberia where it was first located. Then there is *Australopithecus*, which draws its name from the Latin *australis*, meaning "southern," after the type specimen discovered in South Africa in 1924 (Dart 1925). The act of naming ourselves as a species, *Homo sapiens*, wise man, is something of a first. To think carefully about what that name might be — a descriptive feature, perhaps, or a geographic reference, as is commonplace, and to settle on wise man, was a bold and brave choice. As discussed, human beings are naming things all the time, but to name one's own species is something rather more remarkable than many people, perhaps most, might ever have considered. Some might even wonder about the wisdom of naming one's own species as knowing or wise, especially given the self-inflicted predicaments we now face.

7

The Anthropocene

This brings me to the second curious episode in naming; having named our own species, we are now on the cusp of naming a geological epoch after ourselves, the Anthropocene. Discussions and debate about the Anthropocene are a prime example of where questions of presentism-tempocentrism, deep time, speeding up, and giving name to and thereby owning something all come together in the push to declare a new geologic epoch. While naming a potential new geological epoch "the Anthropocene" involves a good measure of owning up and accepting responsibility for undesirable consequences, there is nevertheless a certain irony, largely unacknowledged, about the anthropocentrism involved in doing so.

First, what is the Anthropocene? In reality, the idea of the Anthropocene means different things to different people; the term is used as much, if not more, in the Arts and Humanities as it is in the Sciences, often with considerable poetic licence. As geologist, Jan Zalasiewicz (2021), and his colleagues highlight, the idea of the "Anthropocene has also become used for different conceptual interpretations in diverse scholarly fields, including the environmental and social sciences and humanities." Moreover, these interpretations are often highly flexible and "commonly without reference to the geological record, and diachronous in time."

In essence, the idea of the Anthropocene remains largely the same today as it did when it was purportedly first used by Soviet geochemist, Vladimir I. Vernadsky (1863–1945), in his book *The Biosphere* (1998), first published in 1926. As John Bellamy Foster (2016: 11) explains, Vernadsky gave us the "first introduction of the term Anthropocene (together with Anthropogene) by his colleague, the Soviet geologist, Aleksei Pavlov, who used it to refer to a new geological epoch in which humanity was the main driver of planetary geological change." In a paper published in 1945, Vernadsky (1945: 8) explained his thinking thus:

> Proceeding from the notion of the geological role of man, the geologist A. P. Pavlov (1854–1929) in the last years of his life used to speak of the *anthropogenic* era in which we now live. While he did not take into the account the possibility of the destruction of spiritual and material values we now witness in the barbaric invasion of the Germans and their allies, slightly more than ten years after his death, he rightly emphasized that man, under our very eyes, is becoming a mighty and ever-growing geological force. This geological force was formed quite imperceptibly over a long period of time. A change in man's position on our planet (his material position first of all) coincided with it. In the twentieth century, man, for the first time in the history of the earth, knew and embraced the whole biosphere, completed the geographic map of the planet Earth, and colonized its whole surface. *Mankind became a single totality in the life of the earth.*

The multitude of voices joining in discussions and debate about the Anthropocene means that there are increasingly "partisan, passionate accounts of what caused the Anthropocene, when it should be dated from, who is responsible for the onset of this epoch, and even what the proper designation of this epoch should be" (Chakrabarty 2018: 5–6). For instance, along with Anthropocene, there are also a range of alternative names proposed, some more serious than others, including Capitalocene, Plantationocene, Chthulucene, and Plastic-ene, among others (Haraway 2016; Moore 2016; Parikka 2015). In strictly geologic terms, in essence, "Anthropocene suggests: (i) that the Earth is now moving out of its current geological epoch, called the Holocene and (ii) that human activity is largely responsible for this exit from the Holocene, that is, that humankind has become a global geological force in its own right" (Steffen et al. 2011: 843).

The recent revival of the term Anthropocene is widely credited to the Dutch meteorologist and atmospheric chemist, Paul Crutzen (1933–2021), whose distinguished work, particularly on the ozone layer, saw him awarded the Nobel Prize in Chemistry in 1995. Crutzen himself noted that the ideas underpinning the contemporary use of the term Anthropocene have been around for some time. He acknowledged the particular contribution of Antonio Stoppanian (1824–1891), an Italian geologist who, in 1873, "spoke about a 'new telluric force which in power and universality may be compared to the greater forces of earth'," which he referred to as the "anthropozoic era" (Crutzen 2002: 23). As Crutzen summarized in his widely cited paper, "Geology of mankind," which really set the ball rolling, "For the past three centuries, the effects of humans on the global environment have escalated." He went on to explain how, "because of these anthropogenic emissions of carbon dioxide, global climate may depart significantly from natural behavior for many millennia to come." Crutzen was convinced that the changes occurring on Earth and in its atmosphere were so significant that it is "appropriate to assign the term 'Anthropocene' to the present, in many ways human-dominated, geological epoch, supplementing the Holocene — the warm period of the past 10–12 millennia."

As reported in *The Economist* (2021) following his recent passing, the story has it that in 2000, Crutzen was at a conference in Cuernavaca, Mexico, when, during a session, the term "Holocene" was used repeatedly. Apparently, he became "increasingly irritated by hearing the term used to encompass both the world of today and the world of the first farmers, a world of a few million people and of a few billion, a world of fires in hearths and a world of oilfields." Crutzen was not comfortable with the idea that modern "humans just happened to occupy their period in the same way that dinosaurs happened to occupy the Jurassic and trilobites the Ordovician." He interrupted proceedings and urged presenters to "Stop saying the Holocene! We're not in the Holocene anymore." To which came the response, "So where are we then, Paul?" or "When are we?" At which point Crutzen briefly hesitated before declaring, "The Anthropocene." Not surprisingly, in academic circles Nobel laureates are afforded some liberties that others would be frowned upon for exercising.

In discussing Crutzen's legacy, it was suggested, "When he spoke to colleagues in 2000 about the Anthropocene, Crutzen had no idea how successful the concept would be" (Schwaegerl 2021). Indeed, today there are scholarly journals and magazines dedicated to the subject. Springer publishes the journal, *Anthropocene Science*, described as "a trans- and multidisciplinary international peer-reviewed journal for addressing various anthropogenic drivers and responses of changes on the vitality, stability and environmental functioning of the planet Earth and ground-breaking solutions for restoring and enhancing the carrying capacity of our biosphere." SAGE is the publisher of *The Anthropocene Review*, another "trans-disciplinary journal," which "brings together peer-reviewed articles on all aspects of research pertaining to the Anthropocene, from earth and environmental sciences, social sciences, material sciences and humanities." While Elsevier publishes *Anthropocene*, "an interdisciplinary peer-reviewed journal answering questions about the nature, scale, and extent of interactions between people and Earth processes and systems." For the more general reader, there is *Anthropocene* magazine, which also sells T-shirts, mugs and tote bags bearing their name and logo.[18] A Google search for "Anthropocene" generates more than 5.23 million results, with 1.52 million added in a 12-month period,

33,700 in a month, 16,600 in a week, 1500 in 24 hours, and 8 in an hour (as at 12 noon on Monday February 28, 2022). Skip ahead 18 months or so and the same search generates approximately 33 million results, with more than 2 million added in the past 12-month period, about 3500 in the past 24 hours, and 10–20 in the past hour (as at 4 pm Tuesday September 5, 2023).[19]

The Anthropocene is described as Crutzen's "greatest idea," and indeed, it is readily apparent that the *idea* of the Anthropocene has very much caught on, particularly among those concerned with the state of health of planet Earth. Not surprisingly, however, earth scientists have largely lost control of the narrative around the Anthropocene, for as Chakrabarty (2018: 9) notes, the idea effectively has "two lives, sometimes in the same texts: a scientific life involving measurements and debates among qualified scientists, and a more popular life as a moral-political issue." In effect, the idea of the Anthropocene is the space—time where rocks and humans come together; it is where deep geologic time comes face-to-face with human world history. It is a space where difficult questions about past, present, and future come together, and those engaged in the debate can have quite different agendas. Geological scientists, for instance, are interested in the rocks but not necessarily "interested in the 'whodunnit?' part of the story" (Chakrabarty 2018: 21). Interlocutors from the humanities and social sciences, on the other hand, are very interested in moral-political questions as they relate to the people who have long been walking over and sometimes throwing the rocks.

Crutzen was of the view that the "formal recognition of the Anthropocene by the discipline of geology could easily wait a few years since it wasn't the official ceremony that was important," rather, it is the "discussion and debate" that matters for the time being (Schwaegerl 2021). A few years is the least we will have to wait, for there is an extensive process that goes into making formal changes to the geological time scale. Nevertheless, despite all the discussion and debate, it is increasingly accepted in the scientific community and beyond, that (1) "Human activity is leaving a pervasive and persistent signature on Earth." (2) "These combined signals render the Anthropocene stratigraphically distinct from the Holocene and earlier epochs." And (3) "These novel stratigraphic signatures support the formalization of the Anthropocene at the epoch level" (Waters et al. 2016; Ellis 2018).

The responsibility for making such a decision rests with a body called the International Commission on Stratigraphy (ICS). Formed in 1974, the ICS is part of the International Union of Geological Sciences (IUGS), which was founded in 1961, and is in turn a member body of the International Science Council. Recognized as the "largest and oldest constituent scientific body" in the IUGS, the primary role of the Commission is to define precisely the "global units (systems, series, and stages) of the International Chronostratigraphic Chart." These units, in turn, form the "basis for the units (periods, epochs, and age) of the International Geologic Time Scale." In short, the ICS is responsible for "setting global standards for the fundamental scale for expressing the history of the Earth."[20]

The ICS itself is made up seventeen subcommissions, including the Subcommission on Quaternary Stratigraphy (SQS). Within the SQS is another smaller body, the Anthropocene Working Group (AWG), which was formed in 2009 and is working to formalize the Anthropocene as a geological unit within the Geological Time Scale. The AWG proposal proceeds along the following lines:

It is being considered at series/epoch level (and so its base/ beginning would terminate the Holocene Series/Epoch as well as Meghalayan Stage/Age);
It would be defined by the standard means for a unit of the Geological Time Scale, via a Global boundary Stratotype

Section and Point (GSSP), colloquially known as a "golden spike";

Its beginning would be optimally placed in the mid-20th century, coinciding with the array of geological proxy signals preserved within recently accumulated strata and resulting from the "Great Acceleration" of population growth, industrialization, and globalization;

The sharpest and most globally synchronous of these signals, that may form a primary marker, is made by the artificial radionuclides spread worldwide by the thermonuclear bomb tests from the early 1950s.[21]

The working group states that, to be recognized "as a formal geological time term the Anthropocene needs to be scientifically justified, i.e. the 'geological signal' currently being produced in strata now forming must be significantly large, clear and distinctive." The group claims, "sufficient evidence has now been gathered to demonstrate this phenomenon." Second, it must be "useful as a formal term to the scientific community." Again, the AWG asserts that the "currently informal term 'Anthropocene' has already proven highly useful to the global change and Earth System science research communities and thus will continue to be used." The search for potential "golden spike" locations is progressing. On the back of this, on May 21, 2019, the AWG released the results of a binding vote amongst its members in response to two key questions. Question 1: "Should the Anthropocene be treated as a formal chrono-stratigraphic unit defined by a GSSP?" Requiring a sixty per cent supermajority of votes cast to be carried, of the 34 voting members of the group, 29 voted in favor, while 4 voted against (only 33 ballots were cast). Carried. The second question, "Should the primary guide for the base of the Anthropocene be one of the stratigraphic signals around the mid-twentieth century of the Common Era?" was carried by the same margin, 29 to 4.[22]

There is still some way to go in the process, but the road to formally recognizing the Anthropocene as a geologic time period is well underway. As Meera Subramanian (2019: 169) explained after the vote, "In the end, it will be the rocks that have the final say." The Anthropocene's so-called golden spike must "demonstrate that there was a globally synchronous moment when physical, chemical, and biological processes amounted to the irreversible crossing of a geological threshold from the Holocene to something altogether different" (Subramanian 2019: 169; Waters et al. 2018). Then it is just a matter of the AWG convincing the SQS that the evidence stacks up, which in turn has to convince the ICS of the merits of the case, which then must convince the IUGS that the Anthropocene is real and should become a new unit on the International Chronostratigraphic Chart. Then we have it, a successor to the Holocene.

Not So Fast

Not altogether surprisingly, there are several criticisms of the AWG's position on recognizing the Anthropocene more formally. Some do not like that it is an act of political "responsibilization," which lays the blame for changes to the climate at the feet of *all* human beings when, in reality, it is a wealthy elite who are responsible for much of the ecological damage (Lepori 2015; Agarwal and Narain 2003). Some are dissatisfied with the proposed timing of the Anthropocene, arguing that "major human alterations of Earth's environment long preceded the 1900s" (Ruddiman 2018). Then there are those who are not convinced, cannot be convinced, that anthropogenic climate change is real, or at least not as serious an issue for the planet as the vast majority of scientists agree. That being the case, the very idea of the Anthropocene is a non-starter for them.

Another line of argument is more in keeping with the general themes outlined herein; it does not question climate change and the myriad issues-cum-crises confronting humankind and the planet, or the science behind it. Rather, it questions the timeframe and the urgency to tweak the timescale. James Westcott (2015) puts it like this; those advocating the formal recognition of the Anthropocene as a geological epoch "are forcing an acceleration of Lyell's dictum…We are now recalibrating 'The present is the key to the past' to read: 'The future is the key to the present'." The concern here is that the "Anthropocene posits a worldview in which humans are not just relevant but entirely responsible for the fate of the planet." The speed of the process points to a "sense of epic impatience about the Anthropocene: we want the potential disasters of the future to be visible now. And we want the right to *name* that future now, even before the wreckage of human history piling up at our feet has made its way into the permanence of bedrock." Westcott (2015) suggests that as "a proposition, the Anthropocene is so compelling (featuring on the covers of *The Economist*, *The Guardian*, *Le Monde*, and *Der Spiegel*), and apparently so urgent," that the "geological hierarchy," as outlined above, is being forced to rush what are usually "its glacial procedures." It seems as though we just cannot "wait to declare a new epoch." Herein lies the rub, as Westcott emphasizes, the "job of classifying this epoch should fall to the geologists of the year 3000 or 4000." As he points out, with the AWG recommending that the Anthropocene should have a start date of somewhere around the early 1950s, this will effectively mean that many people living today, especially older generations, will be in the curious position of straddling two different geological epochs (Kjørstad 2022). This would be truly unprecedented.

For some much-needed perspective, it is worth recapping the epochs that make up the Cenozoic Era, the current geological era, which accounts for 66 million years of Earth's history. The Holocene takes in the past 11,700 years. The Pleistocene runs 2,580,000 to 11,700 years ago. The Pliocene accounts for 5.333 million to 2.58 million years before the present. The Miocene

23.03 to 5.333 million years ago. The Oligocene 33.9 million to 23 million years BP. The Eocene 56 to 33.9 million years ago. The Paleocene 66 to 56 million years ago. If the Holocene is to give way to the Anthropocene, at 11,700 years, it will be the briefest epoch on record, roughly 220 times shorter than its precursor, the Pleistocene, which runs for more than 2.5 million years. The epoch in which we now live, which was only named in the mid-nineteenth century by Paul Gervaise, is on course to be superseded by the Anthropocene, barely 140 years after his passing. Even though we are talking thousands of years, on the geologic time scale, this is an example of humankind's need for speed, to make things happen now.

Peter Brannen (2019a) makes some similar observations, noting that geology "typically deals with mile-thick packages of rock stacked up over tens of millions of years, wherein entire mountain ranges are born and weather away to nothing within a single unit of time." It is a field in which "extremely precise rock dates — single-frame snapshots from deep time — can come with 50,000-year error bars, a span almost 10 times as long as all of recorded human history." This makes him wonder, "If having an epoch shorter than an error bar seems strange, well, so is the Anthropocene." Brannen goes on to argue that the idea of the Anthropocene as a geological epoch "is a profoundly optimistic one," for it suggests that humankind will continue living long "into the future as an industrial technological civilization on something like a geological timescale." He was clearly not convinced, for in order to do so, humankind must quickly learn how to adapt and "endure on this planet, and on a scale far beyond" what has been achieved to date, otherwise the "detritus of civilization will be quickly devoured by the maw of deep time."

In short, he insists that we have not "earned an Anthropocene epoch yet." Rather, why not, at least for the time being, consider using another term in the geological lexicon to describe what is currently occurring, that is, an *event*. This is a suggestion that more than a few scientists agree with (Edwards et al. 2022). Examples of events include the Great Ordovician Biodiversification Event, and the Great Oxidation Event, whereby events are "transformative, planet-changing paroxysms," which, with a timeframe in the order of "only a few tens of thousands, to hundreds of thousands of years" are, in the grand scheme of geological time, "blisteringly short" (Brannen 2019a; Ager 1993).

Yet, the idea of the Anthropocene remains a tantalizing prospect; even Brannen (2019b) has been convinced after talking it over with a member of the AWG, Scott Wing, a Research Geologist and Curator of Paleobotany at the Smithsonian National Museum of Natural History. For Wing and other members of the AWG, the idea of the Anthropocene suggests neither a "hopeful future" nor a "catastrophic future." The Working Group is of the view that even if "we wipe ourselves out tomorrow it will still be the Anthropocene a million years from now, even if very little of our works remain" (Brannen 2019b). (This scenario is hard to imagine given the likely event that our successors show a similar thirst for ringing the changes and bringing about the end of the Anthropocene.) The Group, therefore, is more concerned with the "eternal mark left on the biosphere," not so much "whether our civilization is transient or not. *This*, they argue, is the Anthropocene." In his discussion with Brannen (2019b), Wing emphasized that his motivation in formalizing the Anthropocene as a geologic epoch, "is not my concern for future geologists but my belief that this is philosophically a good thing to do because it makes people think about something that they otherwise wouldn't think about." It is curious that Wing should be convinced that the Anthropocene would last a million years or more, while its predecessor, the Holocene, covers a relatively brief 11,700 years. It is difficult not to think that there is a significant dose of anthropocentrism and tempocentrism at work here.

Nevertheless, while one can appreciate the sentiment, Wing and his colleagues are members of the Anthropocene Working Group because of their experience and expertise as geologists, not as ethicists or moral philosophers. If rewriting the rules for how we understand and measure deep geologic time, something very few people are even aware of, is required to get people thinking seriously and changing their habits for the good of the Earth, then we are probably in real trouble. Wing is correct, though, in that the idea of the Anthropocene as it relates to the moral and political debate that goes well beyond the geological sciences, has indeed motivated some people, perhaps many, to think and act. Even some governments have been moved to adopt targets and change long-standing practices, while others that are more obstinate are being sidelined, worked around, and rendered increasingly irrelevant. Perhaps, then, the idea of the Anthropocene is more relevant, and more useful, to pop culture than to stratigraphy (Autin and Holbrook 2012). Or as Chakrabarty (2018: 20) explains, the "Anthropocene, so long as it is seen as a measure of humans' impact on the planet, can have only plural beginnings and must remain an informal rather than a formal category of geology, capable of bearing multiple stories about human institutions and morality. The issue cannot be separated from political and moral concerns."

So why the urgent need to meddle with the Chronostratigraphic Chart? The idea of the Anthropocene fits with the belief that the here and now, especially the now is somehow special, somehow unique, a key moment in history. This in part explains the Anthropocene Working Group's recommendation to go with stratigraphic signals from the mid-twentieth century, rather than the markers of the industrial revolution and European colonial expansion that hang over the seventeenth and eighteenth centuries. The idea of the Anthropocene says more about humankind's impulse to own and name, to lay claim to things than we are prepared to admit. The formalization of the

Anthropocene is a live-and-kicking example of presentism-tempocentrism at work. It is a demonstration of the urge to speed things up, even deep time, in order to declare a new geologic epoch named after ourselves.

Given the relative brevity of its predecessor, the Holocene, how long might we expect the Anthropocene to last before we start looking for signs of yet another geological epoch? Five thousand years? Five hundred years? Rather astonishingly, a Google search for the phrase "post-Anthropocene" generates approximately 10.5 million results, with about 11,000 added in the past week (as of September 5, 2023). While the term means many different things to many different people, probably none of them geologists with an interest in stratigraphy, the fact that some are already thinking of what comes *after* the Anthropocene is both curious and instructive. It is also more than a little concerning. Among those who have pondered what comes next is the noted scientist and environmentalist, James Lovelock (1919–2022), who gave us the Gaia hypothesis (Lovelock 1979). As he approached the end of his life and reflected, Lovelock (2020) suggested that after three hundred years, the Anthropocene was in fact coming to an end and giving way to a new age, the Novacene, a time when artificial intelligence systems are integral to life on Earth and beyond.

Sure enough, artificial intelligence, or AI, is indeed creating a bit of a moral panic among various sections of the community at present, higher education among them. More is the point though; the real issue here is not so much about identifying, defining, and naming a new geological epoch. Rather, the most pressing concern is addressing and acting on the issues-cum-crises that the idea of the Anthropocene has vividly brought to light. We do not need a formal start date, be it the mid-1950s or the middle of the eighteenth century, to know that something must change.

8

Why Now? What Next?

The Anthropocene is just one, albeit it a highly significant manifestation, of the "now is unique" mode of thinking. As discussed above, another significant manifestation is the End of History argument that ensued following the end of the Cold War and its associated ideological battles over free markets versus tightly controlled centrally planned economies. When the Berlin Wall was torn down in late 1989, political scientist, Francis Fukuyama, (1989, 1992) argued it represented the "End of History." This mode of thinking begs the question: Why now? Why do we think now is so special? A turning point in history. The End of History. Worthy of a new geological epoch. Something so significant and so obvious that we can declare it and name it now. There is no need to wait for the passage of time for a bit of perspective, the benefit of hindsight.

As was touched upon in opening up this discussion, there is the living in the now sentiment, which includes some branches of Buddhism. A prominent example is Eckhart Tolle's, *The Power of Now* (2004), which he begins by suggesting, "Since ancient times, spiritual masters of all traditions have pointed to the Now as the key to the spiritual dimension." He also emphasizes that in his life he has "little use for the past and rarely think[s] about it." A promotional blurb for the book explains that Tolle "awakens readers to their role as a creator of pain and shows them how to have a pain-free identity by living fully in the present." Personally, I am skeptical about the merits of living without reflecting on the past, considering what might have been done differently; there are lessons to be learned from past mistakes. Even better, lessons from not making mistakes.

In a similar vein, Dan Millman (1993: 362) identifies a number of supposed laws for living by, including one that he calls "The Law of the Present Moment." He begins this section of his book with an epigraph from Johann Wolfgang von Goethe (1749–1832): "Time doesn't exist; what we refer to as 'past' and 'future' have no reality except in our own mental constructs. The idea of time is a convention of thought and language, a social agreement; in truth, we only have this moment. The present moment is a powerful goddess." Without discussing the context or deeper meaning of what Goethe might have been alluding to, Millman proceeds to outline the path to personal growth, a key plank of which is living in the present moment.[23]

The idea of living exclusively "in the moment" asks one to shed all of life's baggage— effectively to ignore one's past, events both large and small. I get that on a rather basic level it urges us to "stop and smell the roses," to make the most of the moment we are in. However, life is not that simple, and it is asking us to do much more than that. Even on an elementary level, life is not that straightforward. Let us suppose, for example, that a stray dog bit me when I was a child; understandably, I remain wary of unfamiliar dogs. Yet, the live in the now sentiment requires me to embrace the dog with the wagging tail that wanders up to me at any moment. Can I do it? I am not so sure. There is even less certainty when it comes to significant life events, both positive and negative.

Whatever you might think about such sentiments, they need not equate to the now being inherently superior to the past or the future, only that it requires one's full attention, or immersion in the present moment. Whatever that might entail. Even the idea that now or the present moment is the only time that is real or actually exists is open to question. A young Albert Einstein (1905/1952) began to cast doubt on such an idea in one of his earliest papers of 1905 with the rather innocuous sounding title, "On the Electrodynamics of Moving Bodies."

Physicists and philosophers alike over the past century or more have continued to call this notion into question (Davies 1995). So, while ideas such as mindfulness have caught on and been adopted as a means to help people focus, and as popular as self-help books are, the now-as-path-to-enlightenment cohort is not so significant as to account for the phenomenon described herein.

A possible factor in the "now is exceptional" way of thinking is the unique set of circumstances that make life on Earth possible. To the best of our knowledge, they are circumstances that are not replicated anywhere else in our Solar System, or the Milky Way galaxy, or even the known universe, home to at least one hundred billion more galaxies. From this understanding, it requires only "a small step from recognizing that our location in space is atypical to reaching the same conclusion about our location in time" (Davies 1995: 259). Therefore, there is thought to be something uniquely special about both here and now. To be in both the here and the now against such astronomical odds, how can it not be special? That is an understandable line of thinking; one Marcelo Gleiser (2023) refers to as "biocentrism," although I am not sure how many people actually pause to think about it in such terms, probably very few.

As discussed above, we now know that, barring any human-induced catastrophes that render Earth uninhabitable, or a ruinous collision with a very large near-Earth-object (Chapman 2004), humankind potentially have many, many more years ahead of us than there are those that we have lived through. Yet, while we are mindful of the past, and wary of the near future, or what Koselleck (2004: 268) termed the "asymmetry between space of experience and horizon of expectation," we seem overwhelmingly convinced that now is the pinnacle of our passage through time. John Schellenberg (2014), best known for his writing on the philosophy of religion, poses a related challenge in these terms.

Why, after discovering the place of the Earth in the solar system, the place of the solar system in the universe, the age of the Earth, the age of the universe, and evolution by natural selection over aeons of Earth's history, do we still need to be prodded to perform the simple act of turning around, to position ourselves to see both forward and back in time?

In posing this question, it is fair to argue that even our recognition of, and discussions about, the idea of deep time are really discussions about the deep past; there is not much talk or speculation on the deep future. Despite knowing that there is likely to be a lot of it to come.

There are of course exceptions such as H. G. Wells (1913: 5–6), who, in a lecture titled "The Discovery of the Future," delivered at the Royal Institution in London in January 1902, suggested that there are two "divergent types of mind." The first and "predominant type, the type of the majority of living people, is that which seems scarcely to think of the future at all, which regards it as a sort of blank non-existence upon which the advancing present will presently write events." The other type he described as "a more modern and much less abundant type of mind, thinks constantly and by preference of things to come, and of present things mainly in relation to the results that must arise from them." In this schema, the predominant type of mind "is retrospective in habit," interpreting the "things of the present," and giving "value to this" while denying "it to that, entirely with relation to the past." The second "type of mind is constructive in habit," interpreting the "things of the present" and giving "value to this or that, entirely in relation to things designed or foreseen."

In reality, Wells (1913: 8) knew very well that most people do not inhabit the poles, rather, the "great mass of people occupy an intermediate position between these extremes." Which is to say, most people tend to live in the space in between, that is, the present, passing "daily and hourly from the passive mood to the active." Wells would obviously be an archetype of the second type of mind, one clearly focussed on the future. Yet he did so with an awareness and understanding of the past, "not in any professional sense [as] an historian," but as someone who "has always been preoccupied with history as one whole and with the general forces that make history" (Wells 1951: 2).

A key reason for humankind's preoccupation with the present is, as Schellenberg (2014) notes, that human beings are largely self-preoccupied beings. Against significant odds, the line of evolution has led to modern human beings, and most of us lack the capacity of foresight to see where or why the line might keep moving into the future. Even for the most imaginative, artificial intelligence, bio-implants, and cloning are double-edged swords (Warwick 2017). Overall, humankind cannot help but be impressed by the long list of accomplishments, both discoveries and inventions, that we have achieved, particularly in the past few hundred years. This effectively renders us blind to what our descendants might be capable of achieving long into the future.

On that score, about a century ago, the English cosmologist, James Jeans (1877–1946), suggested that, "while it has to be admitted that accidents may happen, there seems to be no reason for modifying our round number estimate of a million million years as the probable expectation, in the light of what astronomical knowledge we at present possess, of the future life of the human race on earth" (Jeans 1929: 341). This led him to speculate:

This is some five hundred times the past age of the earth, and over three million times the period through which humanity has so far existed on earth. Let us try to see these times in their proper proportion by the help of yet another simple model. Take a postage-stamp, and stick it on to a penny. Now climb Cleopatra's needle and lay the penny flat, postage-stamp upper-most, on top of the obelisk. The height of the whole structure may be taken to represent the time that has elapsed since the earth was born. On this scale, the thickness of the penny and postage-stamp together represents the time that man has lived on earth. The thickness of the postage-stamp represents the time he has been civilized, the thickness of the penny representing the time he lived in an uncivilized state. Now stick another postage-stamp on top of the first to represent the next 5000 years of civilisation, and keep sticking on postage-stamps until you have a pile as high as Mont Blanc. Even now the pile forms an inadequate representation of the length of the future which, so far as astronomy can see, probably stretches before civilized humanity. The first postage-stamp was the past of civilisation; the column higher than Mont Blanc is its future. Or, to look at it in another way, the first postage-stamp represents what man has already achieved; the pile which out-tops Mont Blanc represents what he may achieve, if his future achievement is proportional to his time on earth (Jeans 1929: 342).

Clearly, Jeans was hoping, expecting, big things of our descendants in the long future that potentially lays ahead for life on Earth. Despite this, as others have noted, one of the key reasons for our preoccupation with here and now is that most of our wants and needs, even our altruistic ambitions, focus on the near future at best, certainly no further off than a human life span. While that might well be so, the nature of current ecological and environmental crises is forcing some at least, to not only think generations ahead, but to act in the interests of the future. As the Wellses and Julian Huxley argued in discussing the scales of deep time, such thinking should not be beyond us; all it requires is imagination and practice. Another rather simple impulse that Schellenberg (2014) points to is that we all want to believe that we live in the most exciting and consequential of times. That is, rather than eschewing the supposedly Chinese curse, "May you live in interesting times," we are inclined to embrace the idea.[24]

Even though we know that the beginning is more likely to be closer than the end, for both the age of the Earth and the human life that it supports, it appears as though we are none too willing to let go of the biblical idea that the end is nigh. In a field which includes such notable literary contributions as Aldous Huxley's *Brave New World* (1932) and George Orwell's (1903–1950) *Nineteen Eighty-Four* (1949), speculations on the future, near and distant, are overwhelmingly dystopian or post-apocalyptic in nature. Sure, some might involve space travel and form-fitting one-piece suits but, largely, literature and cinema are overwhelmingly inclined to depict a future where progress has violently come to an end and the human condition has regressed from the supposed heights of now to its more primitive roots, eking out a living in some kind of Hobbesian survival mode. The list goes on, from *Blade Runner* (1982) to *The LEGO Movie* (2014), *Metropolis* (1927) to *Mad Max* (1979), *Planet of the Apes* (1968) to *X-Men: Days of Future Past* (2014), and so many more. Moreover, the same is true of some current affairs commentators who see nothing but a "coming anarchy" on the horizon (Kaplan 1994).

Even when people of science come to speculating on the future and the potential wonders of science and technology, such as the Astronomer Royal, Martin Rees (2018: 12–13), they too hedge their bets, warning that we will be "lucky to avoid devastating breakdowns." While the science and technology that promises so much also "empowers us more and more," at the same time, it also "exposes us to novel vulnerabilities." In the process of engaging in calculated speculations, many of these scientists are unable to get away from the idea that, despite the "vastly extended perspective" provided by our growing understanding of deep time, "this century is special," with the "stakes higher than ever before," insisting that "what happens this century will resonate for thousands of years." Why? Because, our "empowered and dominant" species, *Homo sapiens*, "has the planet's future in its hands" (Rees 2018, vii, 3). Okay, we have made a bit of a mess of the planet, but I cannot help but think that this statement is infused with both anthropocentrism and tempocentrism. The planet will survive without us — *Homo sapiens* and whatever other species we might take down with us — and, in time, it will recover (Boulter 2002; Weisman 2007; Zalasiewicz 2008).

Wells (1913: 54), too, even with his futurist hat on, had to "admit that it is impossible to show why certain things should not utterly destroy and end the entire human race and story, why night should not presently come down and make all our dreams and efforts vain." He went on to argue, for example, that it is not beyond the realm of possibility "that some great unexpected mass of matter should presently rush upon us out of space, whirl sun and planets aside like dead leaves before the breeze, and collide with and utterly destroy every spark of life upon this earth." He thought it "conceivable, too, that some pestilence may presently appear, some new disease, that will destroy, not 10 or 15 or 20 per cent of the earth's inhabitants as pestilences have done in the past, but 100 per cent; and so end our race." Other threats might come in the form of "new animals to prey upon us by land and sea, and there may come some drug or a wrecking madness into the minds of men." Finally, of course, he acknowledged the "reasonable certainty that this sun of ours must radiate itself toward extinction; that, at least, must happen" (Wells 1913: 55). Wells seems to have covered most of the usual suspects of doom and destruction, apart from humankind's own ruinous actions.

Despite all the pessimism, persisting with the blinding, even blinkering belief in the pre-eminence or superiority of now over a savage past and a dystopian future severely stunts our thinking and imagining on what might lie ahead. As Robert Textor (2005:17) poignantly highlights, "Tempocentrism makes it harder to pay critical yet imaginative attention to future possibilities and probabilities, and hence harder for individuals, communities or societies to realize future opportunities and avoid future dangers." We have great faith in the idea of progress, are convinced that humankind is steadily improving,[25] and yet, can we really be so vain as to believe that we have now reached the end of the line? How so? More importantly, why so?

It will come as little surprise that Alvin Toffler (1970: 245) lamented that there is not a "literature of the future" that we can call upon for guidance. However, he was energized by the fact that "we do have a literature *about* the future, consisting not only of the great utopias but also of contemporary science fiction." Again, he lamented the fact that "science fiction is held in low regard as a branch of literature," and he thought, despite literary giants like Wells and Huxley, "perhaps it deserves this critical contempt." Nevertheless, he also thought,

[I]f we view it as a kind of sociology of the future, rather than as literature, science fiction has immense value as a mind-stretching force for the creation of the habit of anticipation. Our children should be studying Arthur C. Clarke, William Tenn, Robert Heinlein, Ray Bradbury, and Robert Sheckley, not because these writers can tell them about rocket ships and time machines but, more important, because they can lead young minds through an imaginative exploration of the jungle of political, social, psychological, and ethical issues that will confront these children as adults. Science fiction should be required reading for Future I (Toffler 1970: 245).

As Robert Heilbroner (1995: 95) notes in his musings on the future, it is as good as "impossible to describe visions that will reflect conditions that have not yet come to pass," and that is okay. The crucial point is that we dare to wonder, to ask ourselves what "is *imaginable*." It is a curious thing how those imaginations work; every night before bedtime, my young son and I read together, needless to say, his imagination is much more alive and active than mine. Every now and then, we read some of my childhood books, among them is a picture book about the space-age Jetson family, *The Jetsons Sunday Afternoon on the Moon* (Elias 1972). Now more than 50 years old, the Jetson family does indeed live in space. It is the late twenty-first century and they travel about in a "space cruiser," taking routine day trips to the Moon, where the family stay in touch using "transmitters," much like mobile phones. Like many dads on a weekend, the father, George Jetson, lies about the home reading a newspaper in front of the "spacevision" (television) and falling asleep. George's newspaper is a printed newspaper, seemingly made of paper, and his spacevision does not even have a remote control. It is half a century since the book was published and obviously, we are not a lot closer to living in space or travelling around in space cruisers, which probably comes as a surprise to very few and a disappointment to many. More is the point, it is interesting that half a century ago, while we could imagine doing such things in the future, we could not imagine remote controls or life without printed newspapers, and while newspapers are not quite dead, they are indeed on life support.

What the future might or might not hold is not the point of the exercise here. I am not about to take on the task of futurist, I am not cut out for it; my young children are far better equipped to imagine the future. That is not to say that others should not try, indeed, have not tried. Actuaries and risk analysts have long been required to engage in a certain degree of guesstimating or speculating about the future. Setting aside the place of fortune-tellers, crystal-ball gazers, and prophecy to the margins of society, scholars such as the English political economist, Thomas Malthus (1766–1834), have long sought to understand, and in doing so, shape what the future might look like demographically and socially based on prevailing trends (Malthus 1826). Following his retirement as a physicist, Charles Galton Darwin (1887–1962) similarly took up the Malthusian theme in *The Next Million Years* (1953), in which he "set himself the task of predicting the future of the human race over the course of the next million years."[26] Moreover, it is stating the obvious that the great Leonardo da Vinci (1452–1519) had a real knack for imagining, even prompting some of the ideas and inventions that would emerge in centuries to come. Rather interestingly, some historians have recently assumed the mantle arguing, "We can use the historical method — whatever our specialization — to train our attention toward the future" (Flaherty 2016; Staley 2002, 2007; Bonneuil 2009). In a similar vein, David Christian (2022), of *Big History* fame, has recently turned his gaze from the deep past to the distant future.

The real focus here, though, is the present — *Now* — and our overwhelming tendency to declare all too prematurely its significance in the wider scheme of things. The future becomes important when it is the present, a vantage point to look back on and reassess the significance, or otherwise, of the historical now.

9

Not Now, Later

So, what is it about the present, the here and now, which it makes it so special? The song by Fatboy Slim (1998), "Right Here, Right Now," repeats the title line a couple of dozen times, suggesting it must have some real significance, some real meaning.[27] The official music video accompanying the song depicts, not entirely scientifically accurately, 350 billion years of evolution in about three and a half minutes, from a simple, single cell organism to modern, overweight male *Homo sapiens*. The man in question happens to be wearing a brown T-shirt bearing the slogan, "I'M #1 SO WHY TRY HARDER." Tongue in cheek, perhaps, but yet again modern man comes out on top; now is as good as it gets, why try any harder or look any further.

Much like the metaphorical man in the brown T-shirt, a good many of us see no pressing reason to look or imagine too far into the future, our needs and our desires are largely satisfied, or go unsatisfied, in the here and now. Hence, our presentist-tempocentric favoring of now over past or future is for no better reason than we are living now. As with Eurocentrics, who believed Western Europe to be fundamentally superior to the rest of the world for no better reason than they lived in it, so too, the present, now, is deemed superior to the known past and the unknown future for no better reason than that those doing the boasting happen to be alive now.

It seems to me that our obsessive need for a prominent, preeminent, prestigious now is attributable to two key elements. The first revolves around our impulses for urgency and instant gratification or, at the very least, gratification that is not delayed for too long. The sooner, the better. These impulses can cut across needs and wants large and small: from fast checkout lanes at the supermarket to the fast tracking of higher education; from keyboard short cuts to short cuts to home ownership; from accelerated reading to accelerated depreciation of tax deductions. As highlighted, this urgency can even extend to geologic aging processes.

The second element is not unrelated to the first and involves our desire, a need almost, to be living in extraordinary times. Conflicts large or small are described as turning points in history, before they have even played out. Political figures who briefly loom large and then burn out, spectacular or otherwise, become temporal markers, dividing pre-Trump from post-Trump. In the midst of extreme weather events such as floods, they are declared "one-in-a-hundred year" or even "one-in-a-thousand year" events, even though they seem to come around every few years, or every decade or so. All manner of events and occasions, from holidays to weddings to sporting grand finals become "once in a lifetime" spectacles, despite the fact that they occur with what is often cyclical regularity. Equally significantly, our own relevance and importance is enhanced by the fact that we were there to bear witness to such extraordinary events, and have the selfies to prove it, as social media will testify.

There is a further consideration worth noting here; as of 2020, around 117 billion people, what we call modern *Homo sapiens*, have been born since 190,000 BCE, around when we first appeared. Given a current global population of approximately 8 billion, it means that roughly 6.8 per cent of the people who have ever lived on Earth are alive today (Kaneda and Haub 2021). That is a significant percentage. The weight of numbers might also partially explain why we think now is more significant and qualitatively different from the past. That said, I seriously doubt that very few people are even aware of such figures, let alone give them much thought.

In his book on the idea of the "Great Chain of Being," a book that introduced and laid the groundwork for what we call the history of ideas, Arthur Lovejoy (1936: 23) warned, "the ruling modes of thought of our own age, which some among us are prone to regard as clear and coherent and firmly grounded and final, are unlikely to appear in the eyes of posterity to have any of those attributes." As he went on to explain, the "adequate record of even the confusions of our forebears may help, not only to clarify those confusions, but to engender a salutary doubt whether we are wholly immune from different but equally great confusions." Lovejoy was prepared to acknowledge that, while we might "have more empirical information at our disposal, we have not different or better minds; and it is, after all, the action of the mind upon facts that makes both philosophy and science — and, indeed, largely makes the 'facts'." Around 90 years on, we have so much more information at our disposal, not all of it of the highest quality, and our judgment remains clouded and skewed by our proximity to events. The sincerity of convictions is often admirable, the motivations often honorable, but that does not necessarily render them any less flawed or fallible.

The heat of the moment is usually not the time for balance and perspective. It is not the time to be making bold declarations or determining the boundaries of geological epochs. The time for that is later, in some cases much later, perhaps hundreds or thousands of years. With the passage of time comes the opportunity to reflect and carefully consider events in historical perspective. The future provides a new vantage point, a new now, to look back on the now of the past and to carefully weigh and determine whether it was as significant as we thought it was at the time. There is nothing to be lost in waiting, possibly even much to be saved, and the chances are that we might not be quite so concerned or impressed then as we are now.

Notes

1. The song was written by Kris Kristofferson and is inspired by a woman named Barbara "Bobby" McKee.
2. On the origins of the idea, see Jacques (1965); for more recent commentary and debate, see Levinson et al. (1978) and Cohen (2012).
3. For a critique of Hartog's idea of Presentism, see Lorenz (2019).
4. For a discussion of the colonial European habit of fitting indigenous peoples somewhere on a continuum of time, see Helliwell and Hindess (2013).
5. The magnified and often very large shadow cast upon clouds by an object or observer in the opposite direction to the sun.
6. See Hegel (1956) for the discussion in question. The philosophy of history is discussed further in Bowden (2017a; 2017b; 2022).
7. Compare with the COVID-19 related "anthropause" discussed in Rutz et al. (2020).
8. See a conversation with James Gleick: www.amazon.co.jp/ Faster-Acceleration-Just-About-Everything/dp/067977548X.
9. Whewell (1847: II, 560) proposed: "We need very much a name to describe a cultivator of science in general. I should incline to call him a *Scientist*. Thus, we might say, that as an Artist is a Musician, Painter, or Poet, a Scientist is a Mathematician, Physicist, or Naturalist."
10. The Oligocene Epoch (33.9 million to 23 million BP), marking a distinct transition between the Eocene and the Miocene, was subsequently identified by the German palaeontologist, Heinrich Ernst Beyrich (1815–1896), in 1854.

11. This paper lists the date as a volume published in 1867–69, but there is an earlier paper published in 1850 in which Gervais also uses "Holocene."

12. See also Burchfield (1974) for a discussion of "Darwin and the Dilemma of Geological Time."

13. See the Northern Territory Place Names Register: "Uluru / Ayers Rock." Northern Territory Government, 6 November 2002. (www.ntlis.nt.gov.au/placenames/view.jsp?id=10532)

14. See Secretary of the Interior, "Order No. 3337: Change of the Name of Mount McKinley to Denali". (Press Release August 28, 2015.) (https://www.doi.gov/sites/doi.gov/files/elips/documents/3337%20-%20Changing%20the%20Name%20of%20Mount%20McKinley%20to%20Denali.pdf) Also see Committee on Energy and Natural Resources (September 10, 2013); and "Senate Report 113-93 – Designation of Denali in the State of Alaska" (U.S. Government Publishing Office, 2013). (www.govinfo.gov/content/pkg/CRPT-113srpt93/html/CRPT-113srpt93.htm)

15. The Russian city of Tsaritsyn, now known as Volgograd, was named Stalingrad from 1925 to 1961.

16. Lenard and Stark (1996) was first published as Philipp Lenard and Johannes Stark, "Hitlergeist und Wissenschaft," *Großdeutsche Zeitung. Tageszeitung für nationale und soziale Politik und Wirtschaft* 1, no. 81, Thursday, May 8 (1924): 1–2.

17. See Gazetteer of Planetary Nomenclature, US Geological Surveys: (https://planetarynames.wr.usgs.gov/Feature/14503); (https://planetarynames.wr.usgs.gov/Feature/5683).

18. See: www.zazzle.com/store/anthropocenemagazine.

19. The numbers here do not add-up as well as they might with the Google data being an estimate at best, but they do serve to demonstrate the exponential growth in the use of the term Anthropocene.

20. See International Commission on Stratigraphy: www.stratigraphy.org.

21. See: http://quaternary.stratigraphy.org/working-groups/ anthropocene along with extensive discussion in Zalasiewicz et al. (2019).

22. See: http://quaternary.stratigraphy.org/working-groups/ anthropocene.

23. On Goethe and the idea of *Augenblick*, or the moment, see Rennie (2021).

24. There is apparently no documented reason to believe that this is in fact a traditional Chinese saying, see Van Norden (2011: 53, 257).

25. Classical examples include Turgot (1973), Condorcet (1795), and Morgan (1907). Extensive discussion and assessment are found in Bury (1960) and Nisbet (1980). The idea of progress is discussed further in Bowden (2009, 2017a, 2022).

26. J. B. S. Haldane (1926) takes an interesting look into the distant future in "The Last Judgment: A Scientist Turns to Prophecy" and Haldane (1927) *Possible Worlds and Other Essays*. Another notable contribution is Herman Kahn's (1976) *The Next 200 Years: A Scenario for America and the World*.

27. The single "Right Here, Right Now" was released April 19, 1999, from the album, *You've Come a Long Way, Baby* (1998). The overweight man in a brown T-shirt features on the cover of the album, except for the North American release, which has an alternative cover.

Bibliography

Adler, Hans and Ernest A. Menze (1997). "Introduction: On the Way to World History: Johann Gottfried Herder," in Johann Gottfried Herder, *On World History: An Anthology* (ed. Hans Adler and Ernest A. Menze; trans. Ernest A. Menze and Michael Palma). Armonk, N.Y. and London: M.E. Sharpe, pp.3–19.

Agarwal, Anil and Sunita Narain (2003). *Global Warming in an Unequal World: A Case of Environmental Colonialism.* New Delhi: Centre for Science and Environment.

Ager, Derek V. (1993). *The Nature of the Stratigraphical Record.* Third edition. New York: Wiley.

Augustine, Saint (1961). *Confessions* (trans. R. S. Pine-Coffin). Harmondsworth: Penguin.

Austin, Whitney J. and John M. Holbrook (2012). "Is the Anthropocene an issue of stratigraphy or pop culture?" in *GSA Today* 22, no. 7: pp.60–61.

Baer, Karl Ernst von (1862). *Welche Auffassung der lebenden Natur ist die richtige? und Wie ist diese Auffassung auf die Entomologie anzuwenden?* Berlin: A Hirschwald.

Ball, Philip (2014). *Serving the Reich: The Struggle for the Soul of Physics under Hitler.* Chicago: University of Chicago Press.

Barjamovic, Gojko, Thomas Hertel and Mogens Trolle Larsen (2012). *Ups and Downs at Kanesh: Chronology, History and Society in the Old Assyrian Period.* Leiden: The Netherlands Institute for the Near East.

Bonneuil, Noël (2009). "Do Historians Make the Best Futurists?" in *History and Theory* 48, no. 1: pp.98–104.

Boroditsky, Lera, and Gaby, Alice (2010). Remembrances of Times East: Absolute Spatial Representations of Time in an Australian Aboriginal Community. *Psychological Science* 21, no. 11: pp.1635–1639. https://doi.org/10.1177/0956797610386621.

Boulter, Michael (2002). *Extinction: Evolution and the End of Man.* New York: Columbia University Press.

Bowden, Brett (2009). *The Empire of Civilization: The Evolution of an Imperial Idea.* Chicago and London: University of Chicago Press.

Bowden, Brett (2013). *Civilization and War.* Cheltenham, UK and Northampton, MA: Edward Elgar.

Bowden, Brett (2017a). *The Strange Persistence of Universal History in Political Thought.* New York: Palgrave Macmillan.

Bowden, Brett (2017b). "The 'Idea' of Universal History: What the Owl Heard, the Angel Saw, and the Idiot Said," in *New Global Studies* 11, no. 3: pp.197–209.

Bowden, Brett (2020). "Frontiers — Old, New and Final," in *European Legacy: Toward New Paradigms* 25, no. 6: pp.671–686. https://doi.org/10.1080/10848770.2020.1760486.

Bowden, Brett (2022). "History as Philosophy: The Search for Meaning," in *Histories* 2, no. 2 (2022): pp.80–90. https://doi.org/10.3390/histories2020008.

Brandon, Linda (2013). "Fast-Growing Trees for Impatient Gardeners," in *Fine Gardening* 147. www.finegardening.com/article/fast-growing-trees-for-impatient-gardeners.

Brannen, Peter (2019a). "The Anthropocene Is a Joke: On geological timescales, human civilization is an event, not an epoch," in *The Atlantic,* August 13. www.theatlantic.com/science/archive/2019/08/arrogance-anthropocene/595795/.

Brannen, Peter (2019b). "What Made Me Reconsider the Anthropocene," in *The Atlantic,* October 11. www.theatlantic.com/science/archive/2019/10/anthropocene-epoch-after-all/599863/.

Brown, P., T. Sutikna, M. Morwood, et al. (2004). "A new small-bodied hominin from the Late Pleistocene of Flores, Indonesia," in *Nature* 431, (2004): pp.1055–1061. https://doi.org/10.1038/nature02999.

Burchfield, Joe D. (1974). "Darwin and the Dilemma of Geological Time," in *Isis* 65, no. 3: pp.300–321.

Burchfield, Joe D. (1990). *Lord Kelvin and the Age of the Earth*. Chicago: University of Chicago Press.

Bureau International des Poids et Mesures (2019). *The International System of Units (SI)*. Ninth edition. www.bipm.org.

Bury, J. B. (1960). *The Idea of Progress: An inquiry into its growth and origin*. New York: Dover Publications.

Cannon, Walter Bradford (1915). *Bodily Changes in Pain, Hunger, Fear, and Rage*. New York and London: D. Appleton and Company.

Cassidy, Caitlin (2023). "Australian university sector makes record $5.3bn surplus while cutting costs for Covid," in *The Guardian*, March 3. www.theguardian.com/australia-news/2023/mar/03/australian-university-sector-makes-record-53bn-surplus-while-cutting-costs-for-covid.

Chakrabarty, Dipesh (2018). "Anthropocene Time," in *History and Theory* 57, no. 1: pp.5–32.

Chamberlin, Thomas Chrowder (1908). "Soil Wastage," in *The Popular Science Monthly*, Vol. 73, July-December 1908: pp.5–12 (ed. J. McKeen Cattell). New York: The Science Press.

Chapman, Clark R. (2004). "The hazard of near-Earth asteroid impacts on earth," in *Earth and Planetary Science Letters* 222, no. 1: pp.1–15. https://doi.org/10.1016/j.epsl.2004.03.004.

Chen, M. Keith (2013). "The Effect of Language on Economic Behavior: Evidence from Savings Rates, Health Behaviors, and Retirement Assets." in *American Economic Review*, 103 (2): pp.690–731. https://doi.10.1257/aer.103.2.690.

Christensen-Dalsgaard, Jørgen (2021). "Solar structure and evolution," in *Living Reviews in Solar Physics* 18, no. 2. https://doi.org/10.1007/s41116-020-00028-3.

Christian, David (2005). *Maps of Time: An Introduction to Big History*. Berkeley: University of California Press.

Christian, David (2018). *Origin Story: A Big History of Everything.* New York: Little, Brown and Company.

Christian, David (2022). *Future Stories: What's Next?* New York: Little, Brown Spark.

Cohen, Patricia (2012). *In Our Prime: The Invention of Middle Age.* New York: Scribner.

Committee on Energy and Natural Resources. 2013. "Senate Report 113-93 – Designation of Denali in the State of Alaska." Washington, D.C.: U.S. Government Publishing Office. www.govinfo.gov/content/pkg/CRPT-113srpt93/html/CRPT-113srpt93.htm.

Condorcet, Antoine-Nicolas de (1795). *Outlines of an Historical View of the Progress of the Human Mind.* London: J. Johnson.

Crutzen, Paul J. (2002). "Geology of mankind," in *Nature* 415: 23. https://doi.org/10.1038/415023a.

Cuvier, Georges (1813). *Essay on the Theory of the Earth* (trans. Robert Kerr). Edinburgh: William Blackwood.

Dart, Raymond A. (1925). "Australopithecus africanus: The Man-Ape of South Africa," in *Nature* 115: pp.195–199. https://doi.org/10.1038/115195a0.

Darwin, Charles Galton (1953). *The Next Million Years.* London: Rupert Hart-Davis.

Darwin, Charles (1903). "Letter 480 to Leonard Horner, 29 August 1844," in *More letters of Charles Darwin. A record of his work in a series of hitherto unpublished letters* (eds. Francis Darwin and A. C. Seward). Two volumes. London: John Murray, vol. II, pp.115–118.

Darwin, Charles (1929). *The Origin of Species by Means of Natural Selection.* Sixth edition. London: Watts & Co.

Davies, Paul (1995). *About Time: Einstein's Unfinished Revolution.* London: Viking.

Eckhardt, Giana M. and Fleura Bardhi (2020). "New dynamics of social status and distinction," in *Marketing Theory* 20, no. 1: pp.85–102. https://doi.org/10.1177/1470593119856.

Eckhardt, William (1990). "Civilization, Empires, and Wars," in *Journal of Peace Research* 27, no. 1: pp.9–24.

Eckhardt, William (1992). *Civilizations, Empires and Wars: A Quantitative History of War*. Jefferson, N.C. and London: McFarland & Company.

Edwards, Lucy E., Andrew Bauer, Matthew Edgeworth, et al. (2022). "The Anthropocene serves science better as an event, rather than an epoch," in *Journal of Quaternary Science* 37, no. 7 pp.1188–1188. https://doi.org/10.1002/jqs.3475.

Einstein, Albert (1905). "Zur Elektrodynamik bewegter Körper," in *Annalen der Physik*, 17: pp.891–921.

Elias, Horace J. (1972). *The Jetsons Sunday Afternoon on the Moon*. Dee Why West, NSW: Paul Hamlyn/Hanna-Barbera Productions.

Elias, Norbert (1992). *Time: An Essay* (trans. Edmund Jephcott). Cambridge: Blackwell.

Ellis, Erle C. (2018). *Anthropocene: A Very Short Introduction*. Oxford: Oxford University Press.

Febvre, Lucien (1973). "A new kind of history," in *A New Kind of History: from the writings of Febvre* (ed. Peter Burke; trans. K Folca). London: Routledge & Kegan Paul, pp.27–43.

Flaherty, Colleen (2016). "Historians as Futurists," in *Inside Higher Ed*, January 12, 2016. www.insidehighered.com/news/2016/01/12/are-historians-ideal-futurists.

Foster, John Bellamy (2016). "Foreword," in Ian Angus, *Facing the Anthropocene: Fossil Capitalism and the Crisis of the Earth System*. New York: Monthly Review Press.

Fuhrman, Orly and Boroditsky, Lera (2010). "Cross-Cultural Differences in Mental Representations of Time: Evidence from an Implicit Nonlinguistic Task," in *Cognitive Science* 34, no. 8: pp.1430–1451. https://doi.org/10.1111/j.1551-6709.2010.01105.x.

Fukuyama, Francis (1989). "The End of History?" in *The National Interest* 16 (Summer): pp.3–18.

Fukuyama, Francis (1992). *The End of History and the Last Man*. London: Penguin.

Gat, Azar (2006). *War in Human Civilization*. Oxford, Oxford University Press.

Gazetteer of Planetary Nomenclature, US Geological Survey. 2020. https://planetarynames.wr.usgs.gov/Feature/14503 and https://planetarynames.wr.usgs.gov/Feature/5683.

Gesicki, K., A. A. Zijlstra and M. M. Miller Bertolami (2018). "The mysterious age invariance of the planetary nebula luminosity function bright cut-off," in *Nature Astronomy* 2: pp.580–584. https://doi.org/10.1038/s41550-018-0453-9.

Ghonim, Whael (2012). *Revolution 2.0: The Power of the People Is Greater Than the People in Power: A Memoir*. New York: Houghton Mifflin Harcourt.

Gleick, James (1999). "Seeing Faster," in *New York Times Magazine*, September 19, 1999: p.110.

Gleick, James (1999). *Faster: The Acceleration of Just About Everything*. New York: Pantheon.

Gleiser, Marcelo (2023). *The Dawn of a Mindful Universe: A Manifesto for Humanity's Future*. New York: HarperOne.

Gould, Stephen Jay (1987). *Time's Arrow, Time's Cycle: Myth and Metaphor in the Discovery of Geological Time*. Cambridge, MA: Harvard University Press.

Griffiths, Billy (2018). *Deep Time Dreaming: Uncovering Ancient Australia*. Melbourne: Black Inc.

Haldane, J. B. S. (1927). *Possible Worlds and Other Essays*. London: Chatto & Windus.

Haldane, J. B. S. (1926). "The Last Judgment: A Scientist Turns to Prophecy," in *Harper's Magazine* 154: pp.413–420.

Haraway, Donna J. (2016). *Staying with the Trouble: Making Kin in the Chthulucene*. Duke University Press.

Hare, Julie (2022a). "Pandemic-hit unis cut up to 27,000 jobs in a year," in *Australian Financial Review*, February 13. www.afr.com/work-and-careers/education/university-jobs-slashed-as-pandemic-forces-students-away-20220211-p59vqn.

Hare, Julie (2022b). "Uni chiefs reap million-dollar salaries, record surpluses as jobs cut," in *Australian Financial Review*, May 27. www.afr.com/work-and-careers/education/uni-chiefs-reap-million-dollar-salaries-record-surpluses-as-jobs-cut-20220525-p5aogl.

Hartog, François (2015). *Regimes of Historicity: Presentism and Experiences of Time* (trans. Saskia Brown). New York: Columbia University Press.

Harvey, David (1990). *The Condition of Postmodernity: An Enquiry into the Origins of Cultural Change*. Cambridge, MA: Blackwell.

Hegel, Georg Wilhelm Friedrich (1956). *The Philosophy of History* (trans. J. Sibree). New York: Dover Publications.

Heilbroner, Robert (1995). *Visions of the Future: The Distant Past, Yesterday, Today, and Tomorrow*. New York: Oxford University Press.

Helliwell, Christine and Barry Hindess (2013). "Time and the others," in *Postcolonial Theory and International Relations: A Critical Introduction*, ed. Sanjay Seth. Abingdon, Oxon: Routledge, pp.70–83.

Herzog, Michael H., Thomas Kammer and Frank Scharnowski (2016). "Time Slices: What Is the Duration of a Percept?" in *PLoS Biology* 14, no. 4: e1002433. https://doi.org/10.1371/journal.pbio.1002433.

Heshmat, Shahram (2016). "10 Reasons We Rush for Immediate Gratification," in *Psychology Today*, June 6. www.psychologytoday.com/au/blog/science-choice/201606/10-reasons-we-rush-immediate-gratification.

Hobsbawm, Eric (1987). *The Age of Empire: 1875–1914*. London: Weidenfeld & Nicolson.

Hutton, James (1788). "Theory of the Earth," in *Transactions of the Royal Society of Edinburgh*, no. 1: pp.209–304.

Huxley, Aldous (1932). *Brave New World*. London: Chatto & Windus.

International Commission on Stratigraphy: www.stratigraphy. org.

Jacques, Elliott (1965). "Death and the Mid-Life Crisis." in *The International Journal of Psycho-Analysis* 46: pp.502–514.

Jordheim, Helge (2017). "Synchronizing the World: Synchronism as Historiographical Practice, Then and Now," in *History of the Present: A Journal of Critical History* 7, no. 1: pp.59–95. doi:10.5406/historypresent.7.1.0059.

Kahn, Herman (1976). *The Next 200 Years: A Scenario for America and the World*. New York: Morrow.

Kaneda, Toshiko and Carl Haub (2021). "How Many People Have Ever Lived on Earth?" Population Reference Bureau, May 18. www.prb.org/articles/how-many-people-have-ever-lived-on-earth/.

Kansas, Dave and Todd Gitlin (1999). "What's the Rush?," in *Media Studies Journal* 13, no. 2: pp.72–76.

Kansas, Dave and Todd Gitlin (2001). "What's the Rush: An e-epistolary debate on the 24 hour news clock," in *What's Next? Problems & Prospects of Journalism* (eds. Robert Giles and Robert W. Snyder). New Jersey: Transaction Publishers, pp.83–90.

Kaplan, Robert D. (1994). "The Coming Anarchy." in *The Atlantic Monthly*, February: pp.44–76.

Keay, John (2000). *The Great Arc: The Dramatic Tale of How India Was Mapped and Everest Was Named*. New York: HarperCollins.

Kern, Stephen (2003). *The Culture of Time and Space, 1880–1918*. Second edition. Cambridge, MA: Harvard University Press.

Kjørstad, Elise (2022). "Will the geologists of the future see that something dramatic happened on Earth starting in 1950?"

in *Science Norway*, December 7. https://sciencenorway.no/
climate-geology/will-the-geologists-of-the-future-see-
that-something-dramatic-happened-on-earth-starting-
in-1950/2118181.

Koselleck, Reinhart (2004). *Futures Past: On the Semantics of
Historical Time* (trans. Keith Tribe). New York: Columbia
University Press.

Kovach, Bill and Tom Rosenstiel (1999). *Warp Speed: America
in the Age of Mixed Media*. New York: Century Foundation
Press.

Lenard, Philipp and Johannes Stark (1924). "Hitlergeist und
Wissenschaft," in *Großdeutsche Zeitung. Tageszeitung für
nationale und soziale Politik und Wirtschaft* 1, no. 81: pp.1–2.

Lenard, Philipp and Johannes Stark (1996). "The Hitler Spirit
and Science [May 8, 1924]," in *Physics and National Socialism:
An Anthology of Primary Sources* (ed. Klaus Hentschel; trans.
Ann M. Hentschel). Basel: Birkhäuser Verlag, pp.7–10.

Lepori, Mattew (2015). "There Is No Anthropocene: Climate
Change, Species-Talk, and Political Economy," in *Telos* 172:
pp.103–124. https://doi:10.3817/0915172103.

Levinson, Daniel J., et al. (1978). *The Seasons of a Man's Life*. New
York: Knopf.

Li, Yang, Aina Casaponsa, Yan Jing Wu and Guillaume
Thierry (2019). "Back to the future? How Chinese-English
bilinguals switch between front and back orientation for
time," in *NeuroImage* 203: 116180. https://doi.org/10.1016/j.
neuroimage.2019.116180.

Linnaei, Caroli (1758). *Systema naturae per regna tria naturae:
secundum classes, ordines, genera, species, cum characteribus,
differentiis, synonymis, locis*. Tenth edition. Holmiae: Impensis
Direct. Laurentii Salvii.

Lorentz, H. A., A. Einstein, H. Minkowski and H. Weyl (1952).
The Principle of Relativity: A collection of original papers on the

special and general theory of relativity (trans. W. Perrett and G. B. Jeffery). New York: Dover, pp.35–65.

Lorenz, Chris (2019). "Out of Time? Some Critical Reflections on François Hartog's Presentism," in *Rethinking Historical Time New Approaches to Presentism* (eds. Marek Tamm and Laurent Olivier). London: Bloomsbury, pp.23–42.

Lovejoy, Arthur O. (1936). *The Great Chain of Being: A Study of the History of an Idea*. Harvard, MA: Harvard University Press.

Lovelock, J. E. (1979). *Gaia: A new look at life on Earth*. Oxford: Oxford University Press.

Lovelock, James (2020). *The Novacene: The Coming Age of Hyperintelligence*. Cambridge, MA: MIT Press.

Lyell, Charles (1830–33). *Principles of Geology, being an attempt to explain the former changes of the Earth's surface, by reference to causes now in operation*. London: John Murray.

Lyell, Charles (1835). *Principles of Geology*, fourth edition. London: John Murray.

Macfarlane, Robert (2003). *Mountains of the Mind: A History of a Fascination*. London: Granta.

Malthus, Thomas (1826). *An Essay on the Principle of Population*. London: John Murray.

Margolis, Joseph and Tom Rockmore (eds., 2016). *History, Historicity and Science*. Abingdon: Routledge.

Matthiessen, Peter (1978). *The Snow Leopard*. New York: Viking.

McGrath, Ann and Mary Anne Jebb (eds., 2015). *Long History, Deep Time: Deepening Histories of Place*. Canberra: ANU Press.

McGrath, Ann (2015). "Deep Histories in Time, or Crossing the Great Divide?," in *Long History, Deep Time: Deepening Histories of Place* (eds. Ann McGrath and Mary Anne Jebb). Canberra: ANU Press, pp.1–31.

McPhee, John (1981). *Basin and Range*. New York: Farrar, Straus and Giroux.

Miles, Lynden K., Lucy Tan, Grant D. Noble, Joanne Lumsden and C. Neil Macrae (2011). "Can a mind have two time lines? Exploring space–time mapping in Mandarin and English speakers," in *Psychonomic Bulletin & Review* 18: pp.598–604. https://doi.org/10.3758/s13423-011-0068-y.

Milham, Willis I. (1923). *Time and Timekeepers*. New York: MacMillan.

Millman, Dan (1993). *The Life You Were Born to Live: A Guide to Finding Your Life Purpose*. Tiburon, CA: HJ Kramer.

Moore, Jason W. (ed., 2016). *Anthropocene or Capitalocene? Nature, History, and the Crisis of Capitalism*. Oakland, CA: PM Press.

Morgan, Lewis H. (1907). *Ancient Society: Or Researches in the Lines of Human Progress from Savagery through Barbarism to Civilization*. Chicago: Charles H. Kerr & Company.

Muybridge, Eadweard (1888). *Animal Locomotion: the Muybridge Work at the University of Pennsylvania: the Method and the Result*. Philadelphia: J. B. Lippincott Co.

Muybridge, Eadweard (1893). *Descriptive Zoopraxography, or the Science of Animal Locomotion Made Popular*. Philadelphia: University of Pennsylvania.

Nisbet, Robert (1980). *History of the Idea of Progress*. London: Heinemann.

Noon, Karlie and Krystal De Napoli (2002). *Astronomy: Sky Country* (ed. Margo Neale). Melbourne: Thames & Hudson.

Norris, Ray and Cilia Norris (2009). *Emu Dreaming: An Introduction to Aboriginal Astronomy*. Sydney: Emu Dreaming.

NT Place Names Register, 2002. "Uluru / Ayers Rock." Northern Territory Government, 6 November 2002. www.ntlis.nt.gov.au/placenames/view.jsp?id=10532.

Núñez, Rafael E. and Eve Sweetser (2006). "With the Future Behind Them: Convergent Evidence From Aymara Language and Gesture in the Crosslinguistic Comparison of Spatial Construals of Time," in *Cognitive Science* 30, no. 3: pp.401–450. https://doi.org/10.1207/s15516709cog0000_62.

Orwell, George (1949). *Nineteen Eighty-Four*. London: Secker & Warburg.

Orzel, Chad (2022). *A Brief History of Timekeeping: The Science of Marking Time, from Stonehenge to Atomic*. Dallas, TX: BenBella Books.

Pääbo, Svante (2014). *Neanderthal Man: In Search of Lost Genome*. New York: Basic Books.

"Papers relating to the Himalaya and Mount Everest," 1857. *Proceedings of the London Royal Geographical Society of London*, vol. IX (April-May): pp.345–351.

Parikka, Jussi (2015). *The Anthrobscene*. Minneapolis: University of Minnesota Press.

"Paul Crutzen died on January 28th." 2021. *The Economist*, February 13. www.economist.com/obituary/2021/02/13/paul-crutzen-died-on-january-28th.

Playfair, John (1802). *Illustrations of the Huttonian Theory of the Earth*. Edinburgh: Cadell and Davies.

Pyatt, Kyle and Liz Wahl (2018). "War 2.0: Blurring The Battlefield," in *Newsy*, March 27. www.newsy.com/stories/war-2-0-blurring-the-battlefield-1/.

Rabheru, Kiran, Julie E. Byles and Alexandre Kalache (2022). "How 'old age' was withdrawn as a diagnosis from ICD-11," in *The Lancet: Healthy Longevity* 3, No. 7: E457–E459. https://doi.org/10.1016/S2666-7568(22)00102-7.

Ralegh, Sir Walter (1687). "Preface," *The History of the World, in Five Books*. London: Printed for Tho. Basset, Ric. Chiswell, Benj. Tooke, et al.

Rance, Hugh (1999). *Historical Geology: "The Present is the Key to the Past": a Study of the Prehistory of the Earth and Life*. QCC Press.

Ray, John J. and Jackob M. Najman (1986). "The Generalizability of Deferment of Gratification," in *The Journal of Social Psychology* 126, no. 1: pp.117–119. https://doi:10.1080/00224545.1986.9713578.

Rees, Martin (2018). *On the Future: Prospects for Humanity.* Princeton: Princeton University Press.

Rennie, Nicholas (2021). "Augenblick (Moment)" in *Goethe-Lexicon of Philosophical Concepts* 1, no. 2. https://doi:10.5195/glpc.2021.43.

Repcheck, Jack (2009). *The Man who Found Time: James Hutton and the Discovery of the Earth's Antiquity.* New York: Basic Books.

Reyburn, Scott (2023). "Obsessed by the Present, Who's Got Time for Old Masters?" in *New York Times*, January 16. www.nytimes.com/2023/01/16/arts/design/contemporary-art-old-masters-auctions.html.

Rid, Thomas and Marc Hecker (2009). *War 2.0: Irregular Warfare in the Information Age.* Westport, CT: Praeger.

Rosa, Hartmut (2013). *Social Acceleration: A New Theory of Modernity.* New York: Columbia University Press.

Ruddiman, William F. (2018). "Three flaws in defining a formal 'Anthropocene'," in *Progress in Physical Geography: Earth and Environment* 42, no. 4: pp.451–461. https://doi.org/10.1177/0309133318783142.

Rudwick, Martin J. S. (2007). *Bursting the Limits of Time: The Reconstruction of Geohistory in the Age of Revolution.* Chicago: University of Chicago Press.

Rudwick, Martin J. S. (2008). *Worlds Before Adam: The Reconstruction of Geohistory in the Age of Reform.* Chicago: University of Chicago Press.

Rudwick, Martin J. S. (2016). *Earth's Deep History: How It Was Discovered and Why It Matters.* Chicago: University of Chicago Press.

Russell, Bertrand (1996). *History of Western Philosophy.* London: Routledge.

Rutz, Christian, Matthias-Claudio Loretto, and Amanda E. Bates, et al., "COVID-19 lockdown allows researchers to quantify the effects of human activity on wildlife," in *Nature*

Ecology & Evolution 4 (September 2020): pp.1156–1159. https://doi.org/10.1038/s41559-020-1237-z.

Said, Edward (2003). *Orientalism*. London: Penguin.

Schellenberg, J. L. (2014). "The end is not near," in *Aeon*. https://aeon.co/essays/why-do-we-assume-the-future-will-be-short-blame-the-bible.

Schwaegerl, Christian (2021). "The Anthropocene: Paul Crutzen's Epochal Legacy," in *Anthropocene*, February 14. www.anthropocenemagazine.org/2021/02/the-anthropocene-paul-crutzens-epochal-legacy/.

Secretary of the Interior (2015). "Order No. 3337: Change of the Name of Mount McKinley to Denali," Press Release: August 28. https://www.doi.gov/sites/doi.gov/files/elips/documents/3337%20-%20Changing%20the%20Name%20of%20Mount%20McKinley%20to%20Denali.pdf.

Selin, Helaine (ed., 2000). *Astronomy Across Cultures: The History of Non-Western Astronomy*. Dordrecht, Boston, and London: Kluwer Academic Publishers.

Shryock, Andrew and Daniel Lord Smail, et al. (2011). *Deep History: The Architecture of Past and Present*. Berkeley and Los Angeles: University of California Press.

Skov, Laurits, Stéphane Peyrégne, Divyaratan Popli, et al. (2022). "Genetic insights into the social organization of Neanderthals," in *Nature* 610: pp.519–525. https://doi.org/10.1038/s41586-022-05283-y.

Slim, Fatboy (1998). "Right Here, Right Now," *You've Come a Long Way, Baby*. Brighton and Hove: Skint.

Spamer, Earle E. (1999). "Know Thyself: Responsible Science and the Lectotype of Homo Sapiens Linnaeus, 1758," in *Proceedings of the Academy of Natural Sciences of Philadelphia* 149: pp.109–14.

Spengler, Oswald (1918). *The Decline of the West* (trans. Charles Francis Atkinson). London: George Allen & Unwin.

Staley, David J. (2002). "A History of the Future," in *History and Theory* 41, no. 4: pp.72–89.

Staley, David J. (2007). *History and Future: Using Historical Thinking to Imagine the Future*. Lanham, MD: Lexington Books.

Steffen, Will, Jacques Grinevald, Paul Crutzen, and John McNeill (2011). "The Anthropocene: conceptual and historical perspectives," in *Philosophical Transactions of the Royal Society A*. 369: pp.842–867.

Stoner, Jennifer L., Barbara Loken and Ashley Stadler Blank (2018). "The Name Game: How Naming Products Increases Psychological Ownership and Subsequent Consumer Evaluations," in *Journal of Consumer Psychology* 28, no. 1: pp.130–137.

Subramanian, Meera (2019). "Humans versus Earth: the quest to define the Anthropocene," in *Nature* 572: pp.168–170. https://doi:10.1038/d41586-019-02381-2.

Sutter, Matthias, Silvia Angerer, Daniela Glätzle-Rützler, Philipp Lergetporer (2018). "Language group differences in time preferences: Evidence from primary school children in a bilingual city," in *European Economic Review* 106: pp.21–34. https://doi.org/10.1016/j.euroecorev.2018.04.003.

Tamm, Marek and Laurent Olivier (2019). "Introduction: Rethinking Historical Time," in *Rethinking Historical Time New Approaches to Presentism* (eds. Marek Tamm and Laurent Olivier). London: Bloomsbury, pp.1–20.

Textor, Robert B. (2005). "Introduction," in Margaret Mead, *The World Ahead: An Anthropologist Anticipates the Future* (ed. Robert B. Textor). New York and Oxford: Berghan Books, pp.1–31.

Thomson, William (1855). "On Mechanical Antecedents of Motion, Heat, and Light," in *The Edinburgh New Philosophical Journal*, January-April. Edinburgh: Adam and Charles Black, vol. 1, pp.90–97.

Thomson, William (1857). "On the Mechanical Energies of the Solar System," in *Transactions of the Royal Society of Edinburgh*, vol. 21: pp.63–80.

Thomson, William (1862). "XV.— On the Secular Cooling of the Earth," in *Transactions of the Royal Society of Edinburgh*, 23: pp.157–169.

Thoreau, Henry David (1966). "Walden" in *Walden and Civil Disobedience* (ed. Owen Thomas). New York: W.W. Norton.

Toffler, Alvin (1970). *Future Shock*. New York, Random House.

Tolle, Eckhart (2004). *The Power of Now: A Guide to Spiritual Enlightenment*. Novato, CA: New World Library.

Toulmin, Stephen and June Goodfield (1967). *The Discovery of Time*. Harmondsworth: Penguin.

Turgot, Anne Robert Jacques (1973). "A Philosophical Review of the Successive Advances of the Human Mind," in *Turgot on Progress, Sociology and Economics* (ed. and trans. Ronald L. Meek). Cambridge: Cambridge University Press, pp.41–62.

Twain, Mark (1974). "Was The World Made For Man?" in *Letters from the Earth* (ed. Bernard DeVoto). New York: Perennial Library, pp.166–170.

van Bergeijk, Peter A.G. (2019). *Deglobalization 2.0: Trade and Openness During the Great Depression and the Great Recession*. Cheltenham, UK: Edward Elgar.

Van Norden, Bryan W. (2011). *Introduction to Classical Chinese Philosophy*. Indianapolis: Hackett.

Vanderbilt, Tom (2014). "The Pleasure and Pain of Speed: Are we willing to speed our lives up indefinitely?" in *Nautilus*, Issue 9, January 23. https://nautil.us/the-pleasure-and-pain-of-speed-234746/.

Vernadsky, Vladimir I. (1998). *The Biosphere* (trans. David B. Langmuir; revised and annotated Mark A. S. McMenamin). New York: Copernicus/Springer.

Vernadsky, W. I. (1945). "The Biosphere and the Noösphere," in *American Scientist* 33, no. 1: pp.1–12.

Walker, Mike et al. (2009), "Formal definition and dating of the GSSP (Global Stratotype Section and Point) for the base of the Holocene using the Greenland NGRIP ice core, and selected auxiliary records," in *Journal of Quaternary Science* 24, no. 1: pp.3–17.

Wallace, Alfred R. (1903). *Man's Place in the Universe: A Study of the Results of Scientific Research in Relation to the Unity or Plurality of Worlds*. London: Chapman and Hall.

Warwick, Kevin (2017). "A Practical Guide to Posthumans," in *Journal of Posthuman Studies* 1, no. 1: pp.61–74. https://doi.org/10.5325/jpoststud.1.1.0061.

Waters, Colin N. et al. (2018). "Global Boundary Stratotype Section and Point (GSSP) for the Anthropocene Series: Where and how to look for potential candidates," in *Earth-Science Reviews* 178: pp.379–429. https://doi.org/10.1016/j.earscirev.2017.12.016.

Waters, Colin N., Jan Zalasiewicz, Colin Summerhayes, et al. (2016). "The Anthropocene is functionally and stratigraphically distinct from the Holocene," in *Science* 351, Issue 6269 (8 Jan 2016). https://doi:10.1126/science.aad2622.

Weisman, Alan (2007). *The World Without Us*. New York: St Martins.

Wells, H. G. (1913). *The Discovery of the Future*. New York: B. W. Huebsch.

Wells, H. G. (1951). *The Outline of History: Being a Plain History of Life and Mankind*. Revised edition. London: Cassell & Co.

Wells, H. G., Julian S. Huxley and G. P. Wells. (1931). *The Science of Life*. London: Cassell and Company.

Westcott, James (2015). "Written in stone," in *Aeon*. https://aeon.co/essays/is-rushing-to-declare-the-anthropocene-also-human-error.

Whewell, William (1847). *The Philosophy of the Inductive Sciences, Founded upon their History*. New edition, two volumes. London: John W. Parker.

Wragg Sykes, Rebecca (2020). *Kindred: Neanderthal Life, Love, Death and Art*. London: Bloomsbury.

Wright, Quincy (1965). *A Study of War*. Second edition. Chicago and London: University of Chicago Press.

Zalasiewicz, J., Waters, C. N., Ellis, E. C., Head, M. J., Vidas, D., Steffen, W., et al. (2021). "The Anthropocene: Comparing its meaning in geology (chronostratigraphy) with conceptual approaches arising in other disciplines" in *Earth's Future* 9, e2020EF001896. https://doi.org/10.1029/2020EF001896.

Zalasiewicz, Jan, Colin N. Waters, Mark Williams, Colin P. Summerhayes (eds., 2019). *The Anthropocene as a Geological Time Unit: A Guide to the Scientific Evidence and Current Debate*. Cambridge: Cambridge University Press.

Zalasiewicz, Jan (2008). *The Earth After Us: What legacy will humans leave in the rocks?* Oxford: Oxford University Press.

Index

McKinley, William 50, 82
McPhee, John 34, 37, 42–3
Mead, Margaret 19
Meghalayan 59
Metropolis 73
Mexico 18, 56
microscope 30, 40
Milky Way galaxy 69
Miocene 37, 62, 81
Mont Blanc 72
Montevideo, Uruguay 38
Moon 32, 46, 51, 76
Mount Everest 47–50
Mount McKinley (see Denali)
Mount McKinley National Park Act 50
Mubarak, Hosni 21
Muybridge, Eadweard 30
Napoleon 18
NASA 50
Native Americans 42, 50
Nazism 51
Neander Valley 52
Neanderthals 52
near-Earth-object 69
Nepal 48
Newer Pliocene 37
newspapers 26, 76
Nineteen Eighty-Four 73
Nobel Prize 51, 56, 57
Norgay, Tenzing 47
North Rhine-Westphalia 52
Novacene 66
Older Pliocene 37

Author Biography

Brett Bowden is Professor of Historical and Philosophical Inquiry at Western Sydney University, Australia, and an international Mercator Fellow in the DFG Research Training Group on Standards of Governance based at TU Darmstadt and Goethe University Frankfurt, Germany. He has held visiting positions at the Centre for the Study of Democracy at the University of Westminster in London; the Centre for Interdisciplinary Research at Bielefeld University in Germany; the State Islamic University Syarif Hidayatullah in Jakarta, Indonesia; and the Institute for Research in Latin American Studies at the University of Alcala in Spain. Brett has been elected as a fellow of the Royal Historical Society (United Kingdom) and the Royal Society of New South Wales. His key publications include the monographs *The Empire of Civilization: The Evolution of an Imperial Idea*; *Civilization and War*; *The Strange Persistence of Universal History in Political Thought*; *Direct Hit: The Bombing of Darwin Post Office*; and the 4-volume edited collection *Civilization: Critical Concepts*. He has also co-edited volumes on international law, political terror, international political economy, and served as Associate Editor for the second edition of the six-volume *Berkshire Encyclopedia of World History*, edited by William H. McNeill. Brett has published more than fifty scholarly articles and book chapters and has been a regular commentator in print and electronic media. His work has been translated into Chinese, Japanese, Spanish, and Turkish, while his research monographs have been awarded the Norbert Elias Prize, the APSA Crisp Prize, and the GW Symes Award. Brett is the recipient of a Distinguished Alumni Award from Flinders University for his contributions to scholarship and the wider community. Beyond academe, he is a State Councillor of the National Trust and he serves on several state health advisory bodies, including some related to health technologies, medicines, and clinical trials. He is also a Justice of the Peace. Despite living with a visual disability, Brett is an avid long-distance walker and a moderately accomplished photographer.

Previous Titles

The Empire of Civilization: The Evolution of an Imperial Idea (2009)

The term "civilization" comes with considerable baggage, dichotomizing people, cultures, and histories as "civilized," or not. While the idea of civilization has been deployed throughout history to justify all manner of interventions and socio-political engineering, few scholars have stopped to consider what the concept actually means. Here, Brett Bowden examines how the idea of civilization has informed our thinking about international relations over the course of ten centuries. From the Crusades to the colonial era to the global war on terror, this sweeping volume exposes "civilization" as a stage-managed account of history that legitimizes imperialism, uniformity and conformity to Western standards, culminating in a liberal-democratic global order. Along the way, Bowden explores the variety of confrontations and conquests — as well as those peoples and places excluded or swept aside — undertaken in the name of civilization. Concluding that the "West and the rest" have more commonalities than differences, this provocative and engaging book ultimately points the way toward an authentic inter-civilizational dialogue that emphasizes cooperation over clashes.

Winner Australian Political Studies Association Crisp Prize 2014

Winner Norbert Elias Foundation Norbert Elias Prize 2011

"Thematically pertinent and theoretically ambitious...*The Empire of Civilization* is a sweeping history of the present... Broad in scope and reach, the book engages with the fields of International Relations, intellectual history, and social and political theory to produce an account that is highly relevant

both to the historical and to the contemporary political field...
Overall, we found this book to be fascinating, insightful
and creative...a wide-ranging, ambitious, well-written and
insightful book."

– Norbert Elias Prize Judges

"Deeply researched, well argued, and readable despite the
density of the material...A rewarding read."

– Canberra Times

"This fascinating book traces the concept to the Enlightenment,
when it evolved along with Western visions of progress and
modernity as many Europeans looked at the rest of the world
and saw the task of civilizing 'backward' peoples as 'the white
man's burden.'...In his most provocative claim, Bowden argues
that today's 'new imperialism'...draws on deeply embedded
assumptions about Western standards of civilization."

– Foreign Affairs

"This is a hugely ambitious undertaking, and one which
Bowden in the main carries off convincingly...Bowden's rich
book deserves a wide readership."

– Millennium: Journal of International Studies

"[Bowden's] analysis will prove fascinating to historians and
political scientists. Summing up: Highly recommended."

– CHOICE, February 2010.

Civilization and War (2013)

Civilization and war were born around the same time in roughly the same place; they have effectively grown up together. This challenges the belief that the more civilized we become, the less likely the resort to war to resolve differences and disputes. The related assumption that civilized societies are more likely to abide by the rules of war is also in dispute. Where does terrorism fit into debates about civilized and savage war? What are we to make of talk about an impending "clash of civilizations." In a succinct yet wide-ranging survey of history and of ideas that calls in to question a number of conventional wisdoms, *Civilization and War* explores these issues and more whilst outlining the two-way relationship between civilization and war.

"This book may well suit every reader...Undoubtedly scholarly, the work is never overwhelming...It is very readable, straight to the point and illustrated with relevant examples or quotes... After reading this book, the relationship between war and civilization will seem clearer...The writing style makes it possible to reach an audience broader than just academic."

– International Journal of Conflict Management

"[M]ake[s] an important contribution towards demystifying and debunking the simplistic view which counterpoises war and civilization and camouflages the fact, whether we like it or not, organised violence has been and remains the vital core of civilized life."

– Journal of Political Power

"Bowden clearly identifies the constellation of concepts that coalesce around civilization and war...The paradoxical nature of this relationship, of growing civilization leading to an increase in militarization and conflicts, is a sharp contrast to the rhetoric of peace that emerges from liberal democratic states. Identifying this contrast is important, and Bowden does this very well."

– European Journal of Cultural and Political Sociology

"Bowden raises many salient points in his book. War in all its fury certainly remains a persistent feature of human relations. The amounts of money societies devote to war preparation demonstrate the high priority placed on violent activity... Bowden's observations clearly remain poignant for today's world."

– The Historian

Direct Hit: The Bombing of Darwin Post Office (2016)

On the floor of the Main Hall in the Northern Territory Parliament is a small plaque that reads, "ON 19 FEBRUARY 1942 AN ENEMY BOMB FELL HERE AND KILLED TEN PEOPLE." The plaque commemorates a major event in Australian history when 188 Japanese fighters and bombers launched a deadly air raid on Darwin. Targeting the flotilla of ships in the harbour and key infrastructure within the town, at least 243 people were killed, with as many as 500 injured. Among the targets was the Darwin Post Office, which suffered a direct hit. Taking cover in a slit trench in the backyard of the Postmaster's residence were Hurtle Bald, the Postmaster, his wife Alice, their daughter Iris, four Telephonists — Emily Young, Jennie Stasinowsky and the sisters Eileen and Jean Mullen — a Postal Clerk named Arthur Wellington, a Telegraph Supervisor by the name of Archie Halls and Walter Rowling, a Telegraph Mechanic. All were killed instantly.

Those killed at the Post Office volunteered to remain in Darwin despite the growing threat posed by Japan as the Second World War edged ever closer to Australian shores. It is fitting that we know more about those who selflessly gave their lives for their country when Japanese bombs struck the Darwin Post Office.

Five Stars "Very readable and well researched. I obtained a copy for research purposes but read…more than I needed to, because it was so interesting. I knew so little about the bombing of Australian towns during WW2 and am grateful that authors like Brett Bowden are writing about them and raising our awareness of how war came to our shores."

– Goodreads

The Strange Persistence of Universal History in Political Thought (2017)

This book explores and explains the reasons why the idea of universal history, a form of teleological history which holds that all peoples are travelling along the same path and destined to end at the same point, persists in political thought. Prominent in Western political thought since the middle of the eighteenth century, the idea of universal history holds that all peoples can be situated in the narrative of history on a continuum between a start and an end point, between the savage state of nature and civilized modernity. Despite various critiques, the underlying teleological principle still prevails in much contemporary thinking and policy planning, including post-conflict peace-building and development theory and practice. Anathema to contemporary ideals of pluralism and multiculturalism, universal history means that not everyone gets to write their own story, only a privileged few. For the rest, history and future are taken out of their hands, subsumed and assimilated into other people's narrative.

"Bowden's *The Strange Persistence of Universal History in Political Thought* is a strange book. It is also a book worth reading and thinking about...It is worth reading, however, first as a history of the writing of universal history, and second as a way to think about the way our concepts of history shape society... [A]s a critique of development theory, Bowden's view is to be reckoned with, because it is hard to deny that he has identified a real problem."

– *The Journal of Value Inquiry*

IFF
BOOKS

ACADEMIC AND SPECIALIST

Iff Books publishes non-fiction. It aims to work with authors and
titles that augment our understanding of the human condition,
society and civilisation, and the world or universe in which we live.
If you have enjoyed this book, why not tell other readers by
posting a review on your preferred book site.
Recent bestsellers from Iff Books are:

Why Materialism Is Baloney
How true skeptics know there is no death and fathom answers
to life, the universe, and everything.
Bernardo Kastrup
A hard-nosed, logical, and skeptic non-materialist metaphysics,
according to which the body is in mind, not mind in the body.
Paperback: 978-1-78279-362-5 ebook: 978-1-78279-361-8

The Fall
Steve Taylor
The Fall discusses human achievement versus the issues of war,
patriarchy and social inequality.
Paperback: 978-1-78535-804-3 ebook: 978-1-78535-805-0

Brief Peeks Beyond
Critical essays on metaphysics, neuroscience, free will,
skepticism and culture.
Bernardo Kastrup
An incisive, original, compelling alternative to current mainstream
cultural views and assumptions.
Paperback: 978-1-78535-018-4 ebook: 978-1-78535-019-1

Framespotting
Changing how you look at things changes how
you see them.
Laurence & Alison Matthews
A punchy, upbeat guide to framespotting. Spot deceptions and
hidden assumptions; swap growth for growing up. See and be free.
Paperback: 978-1-78279-689-3 ebook: 978-1-78279-822-4

Is There an Afterlife?
David Fontana
Is there an Afterlife? If so what is it like? How do Western ideas
of the afterlife compare with Eastern? David Fontana presents the
historical and contemporary evidence for survival of
physical death.
Paperback: 978-1-90381-690-5

Nothing Matters
a book about nothing
Ronald Green
Thinking about Nothing opens the world to everything by
illuminating new angles to old problems and stimulating new
ways of thinking.
Paperback: 978-1-84694-707-0 ebook: 978-1-78099-016-3

Panpsychism
The Philosophy of the Sensuous Cosmos
Peter Ells
Are free will and mind chimeras? This book, anti-materialistic but
respecting science, answers: No! Mind is foundational
to all existence.
Paperback: 978-1-84694-505-2 ebook: 978-1-78099-018-7

Punk Science
Inside the Mind of God
Manjir Samanta-Laughton
Many have experienced unexplainable phenomena; God, psychic
abilities, extraordinary healing and angelic encounters. Can
cutting-edge science actually explain phenomena
previously thought of as 'paranormal'?
Paperback: 978-1-90504-793-2

The Vagabond Spirit of Poetry
Edward Clarke
Spend time with the wisest poets of the modern age and of the
past, and let Edward Clarke remind you of the importance of
poetry in our industrialized world.
Paperback: 978-1-78279-370-0 ebook: 978-1-78279-369-4

Readers of ebooks can buy or view any of these bestsellers by
clicking on the live link in the title. Most titles are published in
paperback and as an ebook. Paperbacks are available in traditional
bookshops. Both print and ebook formats are available online.
Find more titles and sign up to our readers' newsletter at
www.collectiveinkbooks.com/non-fiction
Follow us on Facebook at
www.facebook.com/CINonFiction